AF712581

To
Min. Dansel Ross

I Love You So Much!

Your Support & Prayers have
Strengthened me through this Process
Thank You for being such
A blessing to me. The Past
Has been gone & your future is Awaiting!

[illegible signature]
2/8/12

my EX Wants ME Back

DON'T LET YOUR PAST HAVE A FUTURE

GP
GODZCHILD PUBLICATIONS

Published by Godzchild Publications
a division of Godzchild, Inc.
22 Halleck St., Newark, NJ 07104
www.godzchildproductions.net

Printed in the United States of America 2011— First Edition

Library of Congress Cataloging-in-Publications Data
My EX Wants ME Back: Don't Let Your Past Have A Future/DeMarcus Pierson

ISBN 978-1-937095-23-9 (pbk.)

1. Pierson, DeMarcus 2. Personal Growth 3. Spiritual Growth
4. Christianity 5. Emotional Freedom

TABLE OF CONTENTS

My EX Wants ME BACK
Don't Let Your Past Have A Future

I would like to dedicate this book to my extended family...
Omega Ministries International Worship Center of Shabach
Though we have had many hurdles and obstacles, we overcame.
Why? Because God has put more in us than the devil could ever put on us!!

ACKNOWLEDGMENTS

The list of people who midwifed this book is long. Being aware that we are all a sum total of all that we have learned from all the people and experiences we have met and had in our lives, no one can claim full credit of any measure of success in any endeavor. This book is no different.

First of all I am eternally grateful to my Savior Jesus Christ for giving me the assignment to minister to people from all walks of life. Without Him I would be nothing and without Him I would certainly fail. I thank Him for giving me another chance. So to God be all the Glory!!!

Though the names of those who have inspired me to write this book are far too numerous to list, I would like to give special thanks to few who have been truly a blessing in my life.

To my beautiful and lovely wife, Joniesha {aka my ride or die chic}. You have been my support, conscience, and encourager from the start. You are the epitome of what a wife, mother, and friend should be. Thank you for sharing me with ministry. You are the Love of my life!!

To my two sons, Micah and Nicholas, daddy loves you so much!

To the one who birthed me into this world and my #1 supporter, my mother, Janice K. Thompson who I love dearly. Mom, you did an excellent job in raising six wonderful children and thank you for giving us back to God. May your life be filled with nothing but complete joy and happiness.

To my brothers and sisters, Andr'e, Latoya, Kimberly, David, and Darrion; Thanks for sticking up for your big brother.

To Dr. Todd M. Hall, Sr. there are not enough words on this page to express what you are to me in this stage of my life. To many, you are one of the world's greatest prophets, preachers and teachers, but to me you are a father. Dad, it is because of you I have become a better man, husband, father, and pastor. This book is a compilation of your teachings mixed with my personal experiences. Thank you for being that positive influence in my life; to push and challenge me to become not just good but GREAT! Failure is NOT an option and excuses are not permitted. ~ Dr. Hall

To the entire Shabach Christian Church Fellowship Family. I love you all and thank you for your continued support and prayers. Pastors, you guys are truly anointed and blessed.

Who can find friends who are as faithful as Pastor Rockmond Leach, Pastor Corey James, and Bishop Isaac Jenkins? You guys are my best friends for life. Thank you for being the confidants and leaning post through every situation that I've gone through.

I have the greatest team of people who have met every deadline to make this book project a success, the DeMarcus Pierson Ministries staff: Kim Berry (ministry partner and God Sister), Eric Johnson (Grapics Art Designer), Nia Pruitt {the Nia}, Ina Miller (Administrator), Rebecca Roos (get 'er done Roos). Thank you for putting up with me with all the last minutes changes. I couldn't do it without you.

To the entire Omega Church Family – It is such a pleasure to Pastor great people like you and thank you for entrusting me to be your leader.

To my personal fitness trainer and finance chairman, Cecil Ford. Deac, I really thank God for you. I look much better now than I did back then. Lol

I am so blessed and fortunate to father and mentor some awesome men of God, whom I call sons. To Adrian (Champion Praiser), Davarius, Jason W., A.J., Greg Jr., Mikey, Jeremy, Chavante', Jabari, A. D. Cordel Dixon, Deitric, Darrell, Kelvin, Carlos, Reggie, Shannon, Gerrad (Big G), and others, you guys mean the world to me and I thank you for being faithful sons.

Last but not least, to the most gifted, anointed, and intelligent publishers that I have ever known, Shaun and Ana Saunders, Godzchild Publications, Inc. Your ability to tap into the mind and interpret the vision of the author is a true treasured gift. Thank you for capturing my heart and spirit to make a dream come true.

FOREWORD

As I sat to read a few chapters from this beautiful manuscript, I recognized that the past has an assignment. All it wants to do is hold you hostage without ever entertaining the possibilities of a "Future!" But Dr. DeMarcus Pierson has captured a formula and a format that if followed precisely as outlined, will help anyone get their release forms to exit Egypt and head towards The Promise Land. I often tell people everywhere I go; " YOU KNOW WHEN YOUR FUTURE IS READY WHEN YOUR PAST WANTS YOU BACK!" Read this book in its entirety because it's a road map and encouragement to anyone who has made up his or her mind to press forward. Phillipians says, "Forgetting those things which are behind..." but you can't forget if you always have an appetite for the yesterday of life.

Dr. Pierson has strategically put components together in this book that I find are masterful and essential. I want to commend him on his approach to helping the modern world find a blueprint on how to exit matters that no longer have the right to be imprisioning people or chaining people to yesterday. Tomorrow is waiting to embrace us all, and to embrace us all it shall! So sit back and take the time to read every chapter. Find your way out and into all that God has promised you, and all that Life has for you to embrace, encounter, and to enjoy. MY NAME IS DR. TODD M. HALL AND I APPROVE THIS MESSAGE!

To my 1st Administrative Assistant of the Shabach Fellowship of Churches. Job well done and many shall thank you for this masterful piece of work.

Dr. Todd M. Hall
Founder and Chief
Apostle of Shabach Fellowship of Church Inc.

INTRODUCTION

You said you would never do it again. You promised yourself that life would look different this season. You've been tired of the back and forth; tired of being let down by the husband, wife, boyfriend, girlfriend, job, weed smoking partners, drinking partners, clubbing buddies. Your habits have become tired of you, and you have finally decided to let this thing go. You succeed for a little while, but the thoughts still remain. The stench still allures you. The numbers have yet to be deleted from your phone. His voice continues to ring in your ear. Habits you said you would never do again, are fresh in your mind. The thoughts still remain. The desire still plagues you. You shout and dance and scream and holler. People think it's because you are delivered. You know it's because you want complete deliverance. Oh yes, you've made the decision to confess your sinful habits to God. You've stopped lying, you told him/her good-bye, you've packed up the others' belongings and almost gave them back to him, but here you are, stuck in this dilemma. In the left hand is deliverance, in the right hand is your dilemma. Do I move? Do I stay? Do I answer the

> ***You succeed for a little while, but the thoughts still remain.***

phone? Do I pray? What will tomorrow bring? Do I go back to what's familiar? What did yesterday fulfill?

STOP!

Wake up. It's trying to convince you to come back. The choice is your past or your future. Choose your future by living into your present. Your EX- wants to keep you back. It wants to hold you hostage. Let's not limit you to just living life in a constant cycle of regret, but let's go deeper into the psychological and emotional thoughts that birth low self-esteem, which opens the gate for manipulation, purposelessness and negativity.

To help you counter the problems you are facing, this book was organized into (nine chapters) to expose the potential pitfalls and deceptions that Satan uses to pull us back into our past. By the end of this book, you will be freed and delivered as you learn practical steps to overcome the urge to not go back. This life-changing book will ensure that your past will never have a future!

CHAPTER ONE

The EX Factor

Therefore if any man be in Christ, he is a new creature. Old things are passed away. Behold all things are become new.
2 Corinthians 5:17

And it came to pass, when Pharaoh had let the people go, that God led them not through the way of the land of the Philistines, although that was near; for God said, Lest peradventure the people repent when they see war, and they return to Egypt. But God led the people about, through the way of the wilderness of the Red sea: and the children of Israel went up harnessed out of the land of Egypt.
Exodus 13: 17-18

For Pharaoh will say of the children of Israel, They are entangled in the land, the wilderness hath shut them in. And I will harden Pharaoh's heart, that he shall follow after them; and I will be honored upon Pharaoh, and upon all his host; that the Egyptians may know that I am the LORD. And they did so.
Exodus 14: 3-4

This journey will require of you one thing and one thing only: truth. In order for us to confront the multi-layered issues going on in your life, we've got to be free to tell the truth. Don't read this book as a help manual for your best friend. Don't read this thinking it will finally change that man that you've been wanting all your life. Read this and deal with your truth. The truth is, your EX wants you back. That's right, your EX wants you back. And the deep folks who read these words are going to try and avoid the obvious. To them, they haven't dealt with certain issues for a long time so they don't see this particular subject relating to them. But if you continue to read, I promise you that God will speak to your secret issues; God will speak to the tug-of-war going on in your mind that causes you to forget your promise and revert to your bondage.

Your EX is a stronghold. Your EX is a nag.

Your EX is a stronghold. Your EX is a nag. A lot of us are dealing with EX relationships, EX partnerships, EX companionships, EX dictatorships. We have EX-lovers, EX family members, EX-issues, EX- memories, and EX lives that we are trying to avoid from keeping us stuck in our past. But because the church likes to paint themselves as being real good, they never get delivered. Because you have friends in denial, you think you're strange. You feel inadequate because you can't understand why you're pressing toward the mark, but the EX's from your past keep calling you by name. They know your weakness. They pry on your vulnerability. They haunt your hallelujah and cloud your thoughts during praise and worship. The very ones who scream AMEN are trying to scream over the guilt of an EX they couldn't defeat last night. Just admit it: you've got some EX situations that really want you back. Things call you by your name and when you least expect it, the EX somehow learns your new address; finds you on facebook; contacts you by email.

You must understand this principle so that you won't limit this book to a topic solely geared toward love and relationships. This EX- factor can apply to many situations. I'm not just talking about EX-relationships. I'm talking about EX-sins. I'm talking about EX habits. I'm talking about EX- hang ups and pitfalls that have kept you locked inside the incarceration of bondage and brokenness. It's the thing that keeps you up at night crying after everyone else saw you smiling. It's the stuff that makes you think, "Is salvation really worth it after all?" It's the thing that keeps you double-minded, always second-guessing yourself. The EX-factor comes in different shades, sizes, and colors. It's up to you to discern what that EX- looks like to you.

NAMING MY EX

Let me give you some clues. Maybe this will help you to name your EX, and thereby free yourself from judging others for their EX situations. Judge not unless you want others to judge you. You see, a lot of us are nothing more than judgers of others because we, ourselves, don't know how to face our own truth. The name of my EX may be liar, but the name of yours might be idleness. So the tendency for the idle person is to spend their entire day talking about how much the liar lies, when the lying person won't face his issue because he can't get over how lazy the idle person is. We do this dance in church, the blame game, the EX-chase, and instead of us facing our own issues, we apply our problems and issues onto others.

What is your EX?

Stop talking about mine and name your own!

The EX is that one thing that keeps calling you by name and asks you at the craziest time, "Don't you miss me?" You know you have just arrived at or been introduced to a brighter future when your EX shows up out of nowhere trying to convince you to come back.[1] The moment you say, "I'm done," it shows up again! Realistically, because your body left does not necessarily mean your mind has packed up and left as well. So your EX plays with your mind until your members line up with the memory. Most women remain in a situation until they are fed up, but by that time it's so late that the damage has settled in; thereby controlling the mental, physical and emotional balance of her behavior. Most (wo)men who stay have become damaged to the point of no return. Some of us will be better off if we finally make up in our mind to leave the entire past alone.

You know you have just arrived at or been introduced to a brighter future when your EX shows up out of no-where trying to convince you to come back.

But we can't. We won't. It continues to call us; haunt us; want us; entice us. It will whisper in your ear in the most inopportune time, "wasn't it better when we used to be together back then?" As soon as

[1] Dr. Todd M. Hall, Sr.

God saves us and fills us with the Holy Ghost, the Michael Jackson song comes to mind: "Do you remember the time?"

EX- situations represent the past. EX –situations represent your average existence. It isn't God's best for you because if it was, it wouldn't be an EX. Thus, here are three questions that I need you to consider as we prepare to investigate these EX-relationships and situations. The moment you internalize these questions and begin to do some real inventory work, that is the moment you can begin to see freedom break through in your life.

QUESTION #1: WHY DO YOU WANT YOUR EX BACK IN THE FIRST PLACE?

You don't know. You don't know why you keep going back. If it was that good, you wouldn't have left it in the first place. But if it was all bad, you wouldn't be tricked into turning around to do it again. So the question becomes, why do you want it back in the first place? This is the thing that left you when the going got rough. This is the business partner who did you wrong even after you did him right. This is the friendship that always let you pay the bill and never reciprocated. This is the drug that only separated you further from your family. This is the church that always gossiped about your issues but never asked how you were doing. This is the boyfriend who said "I love you" in the daytime but hit you out of anger at night. This is the job that offered everybody a promotion but you, and now after you finally quit, they want to see what they can do to keep you. So, why? Why are you running back to average? Why are you settling for an EX? What is it about you that has accepted lower than God's best for your life?

One reason we go back is because we become afraid that we can't do anything better. We become afraid of our environment. We are afraid that we can't do better than where we are right now. So we revert to our comfort zone. We grow comfortable to the things that gave us assurance. Yes, he beat me but at least he's buying me food. At least I am making some money. It keeps you at the level of mediocrity and you begin to make excuses. The truth is, you're afraid to pursue more. The truth is, your environment doesn't match the potential within you. The truth is, the greater part of God's purpose within you is dying because you won't let God expand your horizons. You've become afraid of the environment and afraid of the circumstances, but when God begins to put something in you, you've got to make good on God's investment. Remember, *Greater is he that is in you than he that is in the world* (1 John 4:4). I may not be qualified for a certain thing, but because I have the greater One in me, it automatically supersedes me!

Fear is a serious setback. We become afraid of our environment, and thus, we want to go back to the comfortable place. My mother lived here so I don't want to leave. My father built this church so if I join another ministry, I won't be living faithfully into the history he started. It is history for a reason, and you need to be careful not to become so comfortable doing the same thing every day that you don't go after God's greater later. There is something greater for you later, but if you get stuck in your EX, you'll never get to the next chapter of your destiny.

QUESTION #2: IS THIS THING ACTUALLY OF GOD?

So here you are. You're dealing with your current situation and you can always see your future, but your EX is always on your mind. *I'm in a present situation right now but my past keeps calling me. My past keeps texting. My past keeps sending me hints that he or she or it doesn't want to let me go. I don't understand why I am in a current situation, I can see where I'm going, but I still have my EX on my mind.*

> ***...what God has for me will NEVER push God away from me.***

It's the same old song, with different lyrics and a hook. The game will never end until you stop and examine if what you had was ever from God in the first place. Women, when you begin looking for another mate, you've got to start the dating season with the question, "Is this for me, God?" Men, when you begin praying for a wife, you've got to look beyond the hips, long hair, and nice dress. You've got to ask the hard question: is this thing actually from God for me? How will I know if it is for me? Because what God has for me will never push God away from me. In other words, the things that God has pre-designed in my life for His purpose will always push me closer to Him, and not to them. Your EX has always left you confused because you feel as if you are in a tug-of-war situation. One day you are chasing after God. The next day, you're chasing after your EX. Your EX has become your primary distraction to keep you far from the hand of God. And this is how you can answer your own question. What God has for you will not only help you, but will continue to show you what God is expecting of you. God won't give you a voluntary distraction to keep you out of his presence. His blessings remind us of the Blesser. When God made one thing, he definitely made another. There is always a greater thing above the good that you are settling for.

When the enemy threatens you with the lies of intimidation or inferiority, it is primarily because he is afraid that you will discover the greater that God has for you later. He is afraid that if you realize that this EX was never really a gift from God, that you will become a threat to his kingdom of darkness. So he works overtime to keep you bound, confused, and deluded; going in circles like the children of Israel. Wasting more and more time asking the obvious questions to obvious answers. Enough is enough!

QUESTION #3: WHAT HAPPENED TO THIS RELATIONSHIP? HOW DID WE BREAK UP?

Every relationship has a journey. Every person in your life isn't meant to be there forever. The reason your EX wants you back is because it no longer has you. Thus, if it no longer has you, then there must be a point in the life of your relationship that things weren't as good as you think they are right now. There must've been a time when you grew sick and tired of being sick and tired. The question you must answer, then, is this: when did this relationship, companionship, fellowship, dictatorship go sour? In short, when did the 'ship' sink? What happened to the 'ship'? We aren't swimming together in the same ocean anymore—what happened to the ship? We talk once a week now and we used to talk every day—what happened to the ship? We don't enjoy one another's company like we used to—what happened to the ship? The enemy wants you to forget the circumstances that made you split, so that you can run back to a sinking ship. But if you can recall the memory of the pain you went through, the tears you cried, and the labor and sweat you had to exert, you will finally be free from the captivity of Egypt.

> ***When things become an EX, you need to examine why it is an EX in the first place.***

So ask yourself right now, before we go any further, what happened to the ship? In other words, why have they become your EX? When things become an EX, you need to examine why it is an EX in the first place. Could it be that your EX got more out of the deal than you did? Could it be that you saw the light of love and let go of the label of abuse? Could it be that you were settling all along and God knew that your job was keeping you locked down? What is it about your EX that gives it the right to remain an EX? Could it be that maybe God did not ordain that relationship in the first place? A lot of times we get ourselves stuck into a relationship that God had nothing to do with; and we did it because we were comfortable in the situation. We went to the church because it looked good. We went to the school because it felt right. We stayed in the relationship because it made us feel better. But it was never God's intention for us to have it. And the truth is, when you step out on your own, you are now out there on your own. You've got to be careful when you start selecting friends that God never ordained. Yes, pastures seem greener on the other side, but when you get over there, it's only turf.

The children of Israel in the beginnings verses were held captive by their own psychological bondage. They had received the signal to go and be free. Pharaoh had finally let them go, but because they had been burdened for so long with the chain of pain, they didn't know how to operate in this newfound freedom. Hopefully, their lessons and these next few chapters will keep you from making those same mistakes. Accept this new season as your "get out of EX" card, and keep it moving. Welcome to your journey of deliverance, once and for all!

CHAPTER TWO

IT'S SO HARD TO SAY GOODBYE TO YESTERDAY

Where I'm Going Is Better Than Where I've Been

One evening while traveling, I sat in my hotel room and suddenly realized that I was thirsty. I remembered there was a machine outside the room. So I proceeded to walk toward the machine. I put three quarters in, selected 7UP®, and the machine read, "vending." The 7UP® came out. I picked it up and headed back to my room. I walked about five steps and to my amazement, more 7UP® bottles began to come out. I immediately looked around. I didn't know what was going on! *You know when something strange happens to you, you look around to see if anyone is looking?* Well that's what I did. Sometimes we feel guilty whenever the Lord blesses us, so we look around because we know we don't deserve it. I said to myself, "Is this for real?" Three sodas came out which makes 4 7UP®s for me? I quickly gathered up the extra sodas and began to walk away again,

You know when something strange happens to you, you look around to see if anyone is looking.

and another soda came out! As if that was not enough, in the coin return part of the machine, there were three quarters along with an extra dime. I say ll of this to say, I put out what I was instructed to put in, and got back more than I was expecting. Keep this story in mind because I will return to this point in the end.

And the LORD said, I have surely seen the affliction of my people which are in Egypt, and have heard their cry by reason of their taskmasters; for I know their sorrows; And I am come down to deliver them out of the hand of the Egyptians, and to bring them up out of that land unto a good land and a large, unto a land flowing with milk and honey; unto the place of the Canaanites, and the Hittites, and the Amorites, and the Perizzites, and the Hivites, and the Jebusites. Now therefore, behold, the cry of the children of Israel is come unto me: and I have also seen the oppression wherewith the Egyptians oppress them. Come now therefore, and I will send thee unto Pharaoh, that thou mayest bring forth my people the children of Israel out of Egypt.
Exodus 3:7-10 (KJV)

"The *oppression,* of my people who are in Egypt, I have heard their cry because of their *taskmaster* [emphasis mine]." I want to highlight something from that verse so that you can understand the bigger picture about your EX. First of all, oppression precedes depression. Before there is a depression, there is always oppression; which means there is someone or something sitting on me – pulling me down, which then causes depression. But the Lord knows what we are going through. The Lord knows that there are some things that you are dealing with. He knows that you really want to change; and He also knows that you want to be delivered; yet, the taskmaster keeps oppressing you.

The Taskmaster

We all have one -whether it's your family, best friend, your husband, wife, your job, the club, the joint you can't put down, the alcoholic beverage, fornication, adultery, lying, cheating, stealing, jealousy, envy, and/or strife. I can continue on; low self-esteem, memories of the past, the secret holding you in contempt and sickness – all of these can be taskmasters that hold us hostage and attempt to keep us from what God has for us. Oppressors are not always on the outside. Sometimes folks in the church can be your oppressor. Sometimes the one oppressing you can be your Pastor. Sometimes, your oppressor is your spouse. Regardless, these are the taskmasters or the oppressors that we are discussing in this chapter. When you are oppressed, you have no control over your direction. You are like the helpless soda can in the vending machine, moving at the direction of another person's thirst. When they move, you move. When they push your buttons, you respond. My goal is to get you to walk away from this spirit of oppression and never return.

One of the qualities that real people have is that they can admit they have some issues, and that they truly want to be delivered from those issues. You can pray for God to handle things real quick, but the truth of the matter is, things did not get to where they are "real quick." The taskmaster is drawing its strength from a bad attitude, bad decisions, and bad choices in relationships. Some of you would be better off in your relationships had you taken the time to really get to know the person behind the mask, but you were moved by the outward appearance. You may have done great, but can your Pastor meet your mate? Are you ashamed to bring him or her out in the daylight? Are you hiding the fine print behind the job description that makes church folks wonder if you should accept that promotion?

What is your taskmaster?

Why are you still oppressed by it?

> ***You can pray for God to handle things real quick, but... things did not get to where they are "real quick."***

IT'S TIME TO GO UP!

Exodus 3:8 encourages me in a profound way. I'm encouraged because I know that God is not only going to bring me out, but His plans are to bring me up! If you are graduating, it is time to go up in life. Why? Because "up" is where the blessings are. Up is where you belong. Many have recently graduated from an educational institution or to a new spiritual level. But what you must understand is that not everyone who has been elevated to the next level is qualified to obtain upward status. It is a horrible thing to go out and still not go "UP." You only get half of a miracle. If you are going to get a miracle, ask God to clean up and remove everything that is not like him and allow you to start off fresh. This may be something that you need to stop and do now. It makes it all better, in the end.

Oppression is the Beginning of Depression

Come now therefore, and I will send thee unto Pharaoh, that thou mayest bring forth my people the children of Israel out of Egypt.
Exodus 3:10

And when Pharaoh drew nigh, the children of Israel lifted up their eyes, and, behold, the Egyptians marched after them; and they were sore afraid: and the children of Israel cried out unto the LORD.
Exodus 14:10

Oftentimes, you really want to get out of this thing. You really want to go up and yet, something just keeps holding you down. Oppression is the beginning of depression. Why? Because before it gets on the inside, there is someone or something on the outside that keeps gnawing at you. The goal is to wear you down in hopes to get you back in the frame of mind you were once in when you had no character. This, in effect, limits the attention you give to the inner process of change, which must develop into an outer manifestation. Don't get it twisted. You can be saved and oppressed. You can be saved and demonically depressed. You can be praying one day and wishing you weren't alive the next!

This does not mean that you have the devil in you, it just means that the devil keeps hounding you to the point that you now feel like there is no way out. Now, because those around us do not know when we are being tested, the process of our change can be misunderstood. Those who live with us, work with us, worship with us are not usually aware of the transformation being birthed within us. This inner work of the Holy Spirit is necessary for us to have the strength to come out and walk away from that which has been hindering us. The things that have been sitting on us will be lifted so that we can live in the freedom of God's grace resting on us. This grace can bring us out so victoriously, that deliverance will become something greater than we had ever imagined.

And they said unto Moses, Because there were no graves in Egypt, hast thou taken us away to die in the wilderness? wherefore hast thou dealt thus with us, to carry us forth out of Egypt? Is not this the word that we did tell thee in Egypt, saying, Let us alone, that we may serve the Egyptians? For it had been better for us to serve the Egyptians, than that we should die in the wilderness.
Exodus 14:11-12

Maintain your Deliverance

Physical deliverance or outer deliverance does not always equate to the inner-transformation. After you are delivered, who will teach you to maintain your deliverance? Maintenance is the issue, not the casting out of demons. Midnight is the issue, not the times in church where you're falling out and speaking in tongues. It is the "aftermath" of deliverance that keeps us wandering in a wilderness for far too long.

The children of Israel left Egypt in a hurry. They gathered all they could from the Egyptians. They got their personal belongings and they headed out. Many times you don't understand how God removed you out of a situation, but one reason you know that you are out, is because those things in your past always send an invitation.

"Do you want to come back?"

"Don't you want to try it one more time?"

The invitation tells me that I am no longer a family member. I have to be invited back in order to be welcomed in! In other words, your past wants to pursue you. It will chase you. Your past will say, "Do it one more time, no one will find out." And if you are not careful, you will start listening to the enemy because it has not been long since you have gotten out of that particular thing. So, your ears are still sensitive to hearing the voice of the past. That leaves you with two things: you can avoid what you hear, or you can keep playing with the enemy and entertaining the situation until it makes you want to go backwards.

Maintenance is the issue, not the casting out of demons.

The past has fantasies of a future based on how you keep coming back. It sees you making the same bad decisions. It's insanity. You know what they say. Insanity is repeating the same behavior and expecting a different result. The reason the enemy is trying to get you back is because he knows he has no future.[2] His fate is sealed and he wants you to be in the same position – doomed. He is after your potential. Jesus said to Peter, "Satan has desired to have you, that he may sift you as wheat." You must understand that the process of sifting requires a repeated action. That is why your past continues to come back. It is the repeated action that weakens your resistance against the next assault. Proverbs says, "When sentence is not executed speedily, it becomes set in men's heart to do evil" (Luke 22:31).

Your past wants to invade your future. It asks, "What are you doing, where are you going, what time will you be back?" It wants to know every step you take. It has no life of its own. History is just that, the past; that which is gone; and the only life your past has...is in your future (Ecclesiastes 8:11).

LESSONS FROM YESTERDAY

Don't allow your past to be led by your tweets. I am not talking about literal tweets, but your behaviors, your phone calls, your drive-bys, attention to your weaknesses and the list goes on. God never divulges the whole plan or all of the details. Paul says, "If the princes of this world would have known, they would not have crucified Christ" (1 Corinthians 2:8). Abraham was called to a place unknown to him. The Israelites were led by a pillar of fire and a cloud. God gave them daily bread, just as Jesus taught us to pray. We do not know the whole plan, we just choose to trust God for leading us into victory.

[2] Dr. Todd M. Hall, Sr.

GOD, DID YOU TRICK ME?

"Moses, tricked us?" they said, but the truth is, God does not trick you into deliverance. Many times we are in denial about how difficult being delivered can be. Some of you have thought in your mind that God has tricked you and made you give up some things. Now that you are free and out and it does not look like what you expected it to look like, you say to yourself, "I did X, Y, Z, and things are still not working out like I wanted them to." Some of you may have accepted Christ as your Savior. The first week felt great. You were speaking to everyone and opening the door and greeting everyone that passed you. Even the animals were given a proper greeting. But later in the evening, you found out that the journey was not as short as you thought it to be. The people were not all that sweet, nor were they on your side when you needed them the most. Have you ever been let down by what you thought was supposed to hold you up?

> ***Disappointment can play on character weakness.***

This can lead to major disappointment. Disappointment can play on character weakness. The children of Israel took one look back and were drawn back to the familiar. Standing on the threshold of deliverance, being willing to stay in slavery, rather than to have faith in the deliverer who brings you out of bondage. Now you are asking God to help you, but you have already set something up that will break the vow. Most of you are tiptoeing back or LARGE stepping back because you have lost sight of where you should be and where you should be going. You were faithful, on-time for service, a worshipper and now you are the one that God has to remind that you made a vow. How is it so easy to pray to God about a thing that you eventually return back to?

Give Your Habit an Expiration Date!

It's so hard to say goodbye to yesterday. Habits that were common to your everyday agenda and formed over the years, you found out that you might need to get closer with God in order to get over those habits. "Yesterday" feels a little harder sometimes, but you must allow God to remove the Egyptian mentally from your mind. The thought patterns that consumed you do not come from the mind of Christ. What you once thought would keep you out of trouble, has not worked because you do not know how God got you out of the last trap. The past is always lurking around. But you have to continue to look forward. Hebrews says, " Let us lay aside the sin and weight that does so easily beset us" (Hebrews 12:1). The word "beset" here means to surround. The past does not want to lose its grip on your memory. It has etched certain scenes on your heart. Your past has planted seeds in your soul that still grow no matter how much you cut them down, but don't dig up the roots. Do not dig up anything that God allowed to be buried. If it's under the ground, leave it there. You have no business familiarizing yourself with dead things. Move forward!

COMPLAINING WILL KEEP YOU COMPLACENT

And when the people complained, it displeased the LORD: and the LORD heard it; and his anger was kindled; and the fire of the LORD burnt among them, and consumed them that were in the uttermost parts of the camp. And the people cried unto Moses; and when Moses prayed unto the LORD, the fire was quenched. And he called the name of the place Taberah: because the fire of the LORD burnt among them. And the mixt multitude that was among them fell a lusting: and the children of Israel also wept again, and said, Who shall give us flesh to eat? We remember the fish, which we did eat in Egypt freely; the cucumbers, and the melons, and the leeks, and the onions, and the garlick: But now our soul is dried away: there is nothing at all, beside this manna, before our eyes. And the manna was as coriander seed, and the colour thereof as the colour of bdellium.
Numbers 11:1-7

The fastest way to continue what you are in is to keep complaining. Complainers love company. They will drain the life out of you with their negative attitude. Just as with the mixed multitude in the highlighted text above. There were some who came along with the Israelites out of Egypt, but they were never in God's plan to come. That's why you can't keep hanging around where you came from; those folks don't know the value of who you are, and they don't understand your connection to worship. Your worship is the vehicle that takes you where you need to go in God. These people do not worship and serve your God. If you continue to hang around them, you will develop an intense craving for what is not in your best interest. Most of these people have no sight of your destiny. How do you avoid this from happening? You must use your spirit of discernment to disqualify any person who smells like, looks like, or reminds you of your past.

DON'T CRAVE WHAT CAN KILL YOU!

How can we apply the phrase, "We remember the fish that we ate in Egypt." That is, how you used to be. What you used to eat and drink.

Don't crave what used to be; your cravings could kill you if you let them.

Do you remember how things used to be so convenient (so it seemed)? Well, God has given you fresh manna and you are trying to hold onto those things that only make you desire the comfort of an imprisoned past. If you find yourself saying the phrase, "You remember when?" too many times, it could be leading you into troublesome waters. Don't crave what used to be; your cravings could kill you if you let them. If it is going to be a flashback, just leave it alone. There are some things that I have not totally been delivered from, and I have to make sure that I do not entice myself to return to those things that "I remember when..." It is always easier for a newly delivered person to be pushed off course if you are not strong enough to tell them "No." Those of you that are dealing with lust and have asked for deliverance, the devil will soon be sending not an unattractive thing, but some pretty things to your sight just to see if he can destroy what God has helped you build.

Watch your leader. If you have a good leader, every time your leader increases you should be able to grab hold to his or her behavior in the process of increasing. Hold on to the same power that God gave them, in order bring to about change in your own life.

Sometimes we have to Lose to Get

Trust me: it can be very tempting to go back when you lose focus of where God said He was taking you. Sometimes you have to lose to get. Sometimes letting go actually allows God to release what's really yours. The quicker you let go, the quicker God can move what's holding you down. If the thing that's been holding you has become a stronghold, God wants to break it. You cannot afford to lose focus of where God says he is taking you. There is a principle in the Gospels that says this: "whoever seeks to save his life will lose it, and whoever loses his life will find it" (Matthew 10:39). That means you have to lose something in order to gain something. This is something that has to begin in your mind. You have to begin to let go mentally before you can let go physically, emotionally, circumstantially, or socially.

Let go in your mind.

Let go in your memory.

You have to begin to change your language regarding what you need to let go of. You have to tell yourself, "I do not need it or him or her to survive. All I truly need is God!" I promise you, God will sustain you even when the need is legitimate, but the means are ungodly. For example, when Jesus was tempted in the wilderness, the Bible says that He was hungry. Satan tempted Him by first challenging His identity, and then by challenging Him to turn stones into bread. There would be nothing wrong with Him eating, because He was hungry. The need was legitimate. The problem was the means through which the need would be met. And that is what you have to be concerned about. You have to ask yourself, "even if there is nothing wrong with what I want, is the way or the timing of my acquiring it, legal in the eyes of God?" Surely God will release what is really yours, as soon you release what is not yours.

For those of you who are aspiring theologians, pay attention to this note. Remember, the enemy never reminded the Israelites that they had just been beaten. Children of Israel, do you remember that you almost did not make it out? Do you remember that you were imprisoned, shackled, and confined? Do you remember the painful parts of your past? The enemy never reminds you of the reality of the situation; he only focuses on the fiction of your past. He makes you crave the halfway good-tasting stuff, but forgets to remind you about how many times you said "enough is enough; I don't want this anymore." The devil is slick. He only brings up stuff to fill your flesh, but he neglects to remind you about who saved your soul. Real friends will tell you who you really are. They will not sugarcoat the truth; they will expose all of the pain, the beauty, and the secrets that you want to avoid. So if you have people around you that are reminding you of what God has done for you, continue in your deliverance WITH them. Don't let them go.

THERE IS PROVISION FOR YOUR DELIVERANCE

God's provision is not always recognizable. We are so trained to lean to the familiar even when it is obvious that what we know it is not what is best for us. Deliverance does not always come in a form that you are used to seeing. Sometimes you have to trust God to provide you with what you need for deliverance. It may not come in the vehicle you are used to, or the place, or the sound. But God will send deliverance to you. There is provision for your deliverance. Paul says, "with every temptation there is a way of escape" (1 Corinthians 10:13). This is God's provision. Nothing will come upon you to overtake you without "an escape" sign or your God-given deliverance. The thing is, we must first WANT to escape in order to see the signs of provision. The children of Israel had the manna for food, the cloud to keep cool, and the fire by night to stay warm. But they stopped wanting deliverance. So they turned God's provision into something that it was not. They yearned for their yesterday, instead of embracing their tomorrow. Find your provision. Seek it out with your whole heart. God desires for you to succeed and conquer your distractions.

Keep God Close

Pharaoh had to release the children of Israel because they were pursuing the will of God. They were on their way to do what God had called them to do. They were preparing to worship; to give God His due; to display His power and demonstrate His glory in the earth. When Pharaoh became Israel's enemy, he became God's enemy. As long as the Israelites embraced Egypt; as long as they were content with the discomfort of making brick without straw, they stayed under the wrath of the Taskmaster.

How many of you are in something that you know isn't good for you, but you have been in it for so long that now WRONG FEELS RIGHT. This is a sign of oppression. It's not normal for wrong to feel right. But Moses' message shifted their perspective. Once they started running after God's will, Pharaoh became God's enemy, and no matter how strong his will was to hold them, he had to let them go. When you allow your spirit to give God praise for your release, you will keep God close. It does not matter if the President walks in while you are worshipping, you will continue to worship while everyone else has their mouths open and hands out to shake his hand. When you are a real praiser, you will praise God until praise looks attractive.[3] "Praise is comely among the upright." That

> ***Deliverance does not always come in a form that you are used to seeing.***

[3] Dr. Todd M. Hall, Sr.

means you look good dressed up in praise.

The Revelation of a Seed: Manna

What is this "manna" that God provided for them in the wilderness? The manna was like a coriander seed. I asked God, "Why did You interrupt the scripture to say that manna was *like* something?" The Spirit then led me to look it up. The coriander seed was an Asian or Middle Eastern spice that was used to season manna. The other quality of the coriander seed is that it releases stress. God opened up my eyes of revelation. In this seed, he gave them something that would give them strength for the journey. If consumed, it would allow them to go through it stress-free!

My point is this: God does not want you to be stressed. He wants you to be free in your spirit, free in your soul, and free in your body. God is not going to allow you to struggle to get out of a thing by yourself. He is going to send help for you. Help may come in many forms. It may not be the help that you envision. It may be a stranger or someone who contacts you and tells you that God has sent them to help you come out. Perhaps you have not heard from them in a while but you get an unexpected phone call. The voice on the other end says, "I've been holding this money, this car, or I will be paying rent in this apartment until God releases me." If you believe God can do this, you will learn to give him praise in advance for the miracle.

You have admitted to having issues but you have not asked for direction. So the best way you can ask for direction, is to say to God, "not only bring me out, but take me up." When you are up, yesterday only becomes a forgotten dream...and you are heading straight into your destiny.

CHAPTER THREE

Loving Two is Hard to Do

If thy brother, the son of thy mother, or thy son, or thy daughter, or the wife of thy bosom, or thy friend, which is as thine own soul, entice thee secretly, saying, Let us go and serve other gods, which thou hast not known, thou, nor thy fathers; Namely, of the gods of the people which are round about you, nigh unto thee, or far off from thee, from the one end of the earth even unto the other end of the earth; Thou shalt not consent unto him, nor hearken unto him; neither shall thine eye pity him, neither shalt thou spare, neither shalt thou conceal him: But thou shalt surely kill him; thine hand shall be first upon him to put him to death, and afterwards the hand of all the people.

Deuteronomy 13:6-9

One day Samson went to Gaza, where he saw a prostitute. He went in to spend the night with her. The people of Gaza were told, "Samson is here!" So they surrounded the place and lay in wait for him all night at the city gate. They made no move during the night, saying, "At dawn we'll kill him." But Samson lay there only until the middle of the night. Then he got up and took hold of the doors of the city gate, together with the two posts, and tore them loose, bar and all. He lifted them to his shoulders and carried them to the top of the hill that faces Hebron. Some time later, he fell in love with a woman in the Valley of Sorek whose name was Delilah. The rulers of the Philistines went to her and said, "See if you can lure him into showing you the secret of his great strength and how we can overpower him so we may tie him up and subdue him. Each one of us will give you eleven hundred shekels of silver."

Judges 16:1-5

The story of Samson is an unfortunate one. It is a sad story because it shows a man who had a struggle, just like you and me. It shows a woman who was paid for hire. It shows a man whose struggle ruined his success. It shows a woman who could care less. But the difference between our struggle and his, was that he exposed his weakness to the wrong person. He exposed his faults to the decoy, and not the God-designed helpmate. He let his hair down one time too many, and the rest is all history.

> ***But the difference between our struggle and his, was that he exposed his weakness to the wrong person.***

In this chapter I want to walk you through Samson's story, in the hopes that you will learn from his mistakes, and vow not to become a repeat offender. I want you to know that loving two is hard to do. It is very hard to love your wife, and love the mistress on the side, too. Loving two is hard to do. It is very hard to commit your life to a career, when your passion is centered on your own business. Loving two is hard to do. It's very hard to give your life to Christ, but still hang around those friends that encourage you to keep smoking weed. Loving two is hard to do. It's like juggling a bag full of bowling pins without the training or the experience. You'll try to make it work, and for the first few moments, you'll trick yourself into thinking that you know what you're doing. But in the end, you will fail. You will falter. You will fall. Those pins will hit the ground; and somebody's life may be in danger.

Samson was a regular man with an irregular power. He was a human being, with feelings and desires and faults; but he was also an anointed man with great strength and agility. Samson was the kind of man whom every woman would look at on the way to the gym, thinking, "I wish I had a man like that around the house to help me with my bags." Everywhere Samson went, he made some friends. But also, he made some enemies. His strength was attractive. Not just to those who needed help from him, but also to those who wanted to hurt him.

Assess your FRIENDS from your ENEMIES

As you journey through your deliverance, you've got to be able to properly assess the people in your life. Everyone boasting about your strength isn't proud of you for the strength you have. Some of the closest people around you are actually envious of you. Why? Because God gave you something that they could not do. You're much more attractive than they are. You're more articulate. You have a man and they don't. You bought your house before they bought theirs. There are loads of reasons why friends can turn into enemies. So be mindful of your close associates; because there is a Judas in every camp.

Samson was strong; but he wasn't smart. And sometimes, God gives us one gift, and we lose our senses and forget about the other gifts we don't possess. So, just because you can preach doesn't mean you know how to live a pure life. And just because God gave you the gift of financial success, doesn't mean that you have the skills to manage money. Just because you have the gift to lay hands on the sick, doesn't mean you should get up tomorrow and start your own church. Be mindful, Samson! Your gift is in your strength, not your smarts!

Know Your Limitations

We need to know our limitations. All of us have them. All of us have areas in our lives that make us realize how much we need someone else. But the problem with Samson was that his strength distracted people from the real problem. Samson loved women. He was addicted to the touch of a beautiful woman. At the same time, Samson also loved God. But, loving two is hard to do.

The bible tells us in the beginning of Judges 16 that Samson had a desire for women of all kinds. Most times, preachers begin his story at Delilah, but the truth is, there is always a forerunner before your true test manifests. Jesus is the Savior, but John the Baptist was his forerunner. In the same way, Delilah was the temptress, but the prostitutes were her forerunners. You've got to learn to leave the first EX alone, because every round goes higher and higher. If you can't get out while the iron isn't hot, you will surely burn up when you bump into a spiritual "Delilah."

Who is "the prostitute" in your life? When was your forerunner experience? How did God warn you about the Delilah that was soon to come? If you want to stay out from the ex-factor, you've got to recognize your weakness in the temporary "prostitute situations"; if not, you will surely be overtaken when you meet a match you can't beat.

Delilah stands for Distraction

Samson fell in love with this woman named Delilah, but just like most men, he wasn't thinking responsibly. First of all, this woman was on a lower level than he was. Research tells us that Samson was from the mountain. Delilah, however, was from the valley. Samson was popular and was given high regard for his commendable personality and gift. But this woman wasn't so popular. In fact, she was from a low state. Their partnership didn't match from the very beginning. But instead of running from it, Samson ran toward this distraction and tried to make it work anyway.

Listen! You will always find yourself back in this place if you keep trying to fit yourself in a shoe that doesn't fit. God gives us ways of escape (I told you this in the last chapter), but it's ultimately up to you to exit when you see "no match found" written on the forehead of your "Delilah." Whether it is a business partnership, a preaching engagement, an opportunity to date someone, or a job offer, you have to pay attention to the signs. God wants you to be equally yoked with every "-ship" that you sail on. Every partnership must be equally yoked. Every friendship must be equally yoked. Every relationship must be equally yoked. The moment you feel seasick, get off the boat! There's a shift in the room, and somebody isn't carrying their weight.

Distractions Come Packaged in Attraction

Distractions come packaged in attraction. They look the part but they don't qualify to carry you through the difficult seasons of life. They sound like the right match, but the true "ship" for you will be equal in stature, strength, anointing and wisdom- and in fact, they will sometimes be better than you. Why? Because your gift needs a challenge. If you are never challenged by your "ship," then why are you on it? If none of your friends are smarter than you, then do you really have friends or are they slaves? Who is challenging you to be better? Who is correcting you when you are wrong? Who is helping you to be accountable?

Delilah knew that Samson lacked the intelligence necessary to distinguish distraction from destiny; but we have something Samson didn't have. We have his story to learn from. We have the Holy Ghost within us that tells us, "don't go there! Don't do that! Listen to your pastor! Leave that girl alone." It's up to us to listen to that voice and obey it.

What You Don't know WILL Hurt You

They always used to say "What you don't know can't hurt you," but that is one of the biggest lies I've ever heard. What you don't know will not only hurt you, it may kill you. The more you plead ignorance, the more room you give the enemy to hibernate in your life to snatch away opportunities from you when you least expect it.

Consider the text again.

Delilah was instructed by a band of leaders. They wanted her to find out why Samson was so strong. She wasn't in it for love. She never said, "I love you, Sam-Sam!" She never made a promise; never made a vow. But he heard something she never said. He put words in her mouth and planted promises in her heart. He wanted her love more than he wanted his strength. You've got to be careful about giving up your anointing for a relationship. You can want something so bad that you miss out on what God intended for you to have. Don't forfeit your future for a pretty face and a few dollars. If you do, you're a prostitute, not a purpose-filled Christian.

You can want something so bad that you miss out on what God intended for you to have.

Samson was sprung. He was, as the young people call it, "beat." He didn't know his left from his right. He didn't know the church house from the clubhouse. Poor Samson! If only he would've realized earlier that she did not love him. He didn't even see it. He was too engrossed by her beauty, hypnotized by her lustful eyes, and captivated by her enticing words. What he did not know did hurt him. He did not know she wasn't there for love. He thought she was seeing him with the same level of seriousness that he was seeing her. But that's how the enemy works—he comes "as a roaring lion." His best work is to look like he has good intentions. But he doesn't. He NEVER loved you. He never cared about you. Satan is a masterful magician. He will deceive you by "the appearance of love," and overtake you by the naiveté of your ignorance. Beware of the people who never have anything to give but always want to glean something from you. Delilah wanted information, but she was not willing to give him affection. She withheld from loving him until he did something for her. She's like a lot of the people you bring into your life. They never offer to pay for a meal. Instead, they are always borrowing, always taking, and never saying "thank you." Don't let it happen!

Samson was infatuated. He was head over heels. And this infatuation allowed him to be used. It's a shame when a man loves a woman so bad that he will let her use him before he lets her love him. Don't let a man use your body. Tell him "love me by waiting for me." Don't let your boss use your ideas. Tell them, "pay me more or I'll sell this idea to another bidder." Don't let your children abuse you and guilt you because you are a single parent. Tell them, "if you think you can do a better job, do it yourself (especially if they are of age)." Stand up for yourself. God gave you a precious gift; and the last thing you need to do, is give it up to a Delilah who never cared about you in the first place.

HE CALLED IT LOVE; SHE CALLED IT A PAYCHECK!

The story continues, but the repercussions get worse. Delilah was told that if she found out about Samson's strength, she would get a significant financial reward. In Samson's eyes, all he saw was love. In her eyes, all she saw were dollar signs.

What do people really see when they look at you?

Do they care about you, or do they care about what they can get by knowing you?

Delilah asked Samson and he gave her an answer, playing with her. He invited her to test him. She used what Samson told her and hid some Philistines in her closet to take advantage of what they thought his weakness was. Turns out, he was just flirting with her all along. So Delilah persisted. Again she asked him where his weakness was. She wanted to know where he got his strength from. His love blinded him of her real agenda. He wanted affection; she wanted a pension. He wanted a peck; she wanted a check. In every relationship, you've got to assess what the other person wants. If it doesn't sound like the things you need to flourish, get out of it quickly.

All this time, Delilah continued doing the job she was hired for. She became more curious about the source of his strength. She was using him and he didn't even know it. You see, it's one thing to use me with my eyes open. It's another thing to use me with my head in your lap. When you use me in my state of vulnerability, you're not just using me...you're ABUSING ME!

She was being paid to be his enemy. And the same is true for some of us. I know you don't believe that people are paid to be your enemy, but I assure you, if God has called you to defeat the plans of the enemy, there are wicked people in place trying to terrorize your faith right now. They are paid to assist in the demise of your life. How do you think terrorists were able to live on American soil, and all the while, plan for our complete obliteration on 9/11? They were hired by American jobs, paid every other Friday, to destroy us on our turf. When you see someone on your job whom you know was sent by the enemy to aggravate your spirit, that's an example of someone being paid to ruin your testimony. The enemy has set out to destroy you at any cost. There is no amount too high; there is no challenge too extreme—to keep him from getting you in his lap. If you're serious about leaving your -EX alone, you've got to recognize the enemy in disguise. Never put yourself in a position to be destroyed by the thing you've fallen in love with.

KNOW THAT YOU ARE ANOINTED. KNOW WHY YOU ARE ANOINTED

Most of us know how the story ends. Soon enough, Samson reveals his secret to Delilah and she conspires to have his hair cut off. Upon waking up that morning, he discovers his locks are gone and with the hair gone, so too is his strength gone. One or two passionate nights of lap-laying and intimate conversation destroyed his destiny forever. He destroyed his life in a powerful way. He could no longer be effective in what God gave him the strength to do. But when I examine this story, I have to admit: I have some sympathy for Brother Samson. I have sympathy for him because he didn't know that he was anointed; and more importantly, he didn't know WHY he was anointed.

Most of us are just like him. We don't realize that the things that make us different are not because we are weird. Those are signs of God's anointing on our lives. We don't realize that being talked about as a child was a clue that God was putting something in us that would ultimately change the world. We don't recognize why people either draw too us all the time, or repel from us, leaving us to find ourselves alone and desiring friendship. But all the while, this is what it takes to be anointed. When we have a gift, and we don't know that God gave us this gift, we don't nurture or cherish it like we're supposed to. You can't be a good steward over something that you don't know is worthy of stewardship. It's like the painting found in the garage, which sold for millions at a garage sale a few years ago. The owner of the painting didn't understand the value of the artistry. So instead of profiting from the painting, he let this million-dollar product sit in the garage and collect dust.

The same is true for us. If we don't value the anointing that God has deposited in us, we will let people use us, kick us to the side, and we will look up one day, and realize that our soul is collecting dust. You've got to know who you are. Know that you are fearfully and wonderfully made. Know that God made you for a purpose and with an intention in mind to shine his best light through you. Know that every gift he deposited in you will be the very thing that brings you into prosperity.

If you praised him more for who He is in you, you would get your breakthrough faster. Why? Because you would realize, "I cannot afford to stay trapped in the garage, inside of a cardboard box collecting dust. There's greater in me that the world needs to see." If you knew who you were, you wouldn't let Delilah have the luxury of placing her fingerprints on your fine artistry. You are a Collector's Item in God's museum of Greatness. Everything you do is anointed. Every thing God says through you is unique. Every time you surrender to Him, the heavens open and souls come to Christ. You've got to know who you are or you will always devalue what God put inside of you.

What makes you do what you do so well?

Why are you always "the exception" and not "the rule?"

Why did God give you this gift? For what purpose?

REVEAL THE PURPOSE OF MY GIFT, LORD!

Most anointed people don't have a clue why God anointed them. They know they have a gift, but they don't know the gift's purpose. We know that we can sing, but we don't understand that our voice is used to shake the very foundations of hell. We know that we can teach or preach, but we don't recognize that God uses our words to shift atmospheres. We know we have a gift to persuade people in the courtroom, but we don't recognize that God has positioned us in the legal system to bring prayer back in the schools. He made us a police officer so that we could change the prison system. He's given us the anointing and the favor so that we can edify the kingdom, and bring Him glory. But if you don't know WHY you are anointed, you will prematurely give your strength away to the highest bidder.

Don't let it happen to you.

Ask God to reveal your gifts and the purpose behind them.

Guard your gifts with your life. Don't fall asleep in Delilah's lap.

Most anointed people don't have a clue why God anointed them.

She was his enemy. She was his EX-factor. She was sent in his life to destroy him forever. An enemy is anyone who tries to sabotage the assignment that God has for your life. An enemy is someone whose words of affirmation contradict their actions of betrayal. If anyone entices you to fall, you need to kill that relationship. You need to detach yourself as soon as possible. Even if it feels good, kill it. Feelings are nothing more than feelings. Even if that means you will take a major pay cut, kill it. God won't let you down. You've got to trust him beyond the salary, the relationship, the connection; you've got to kill anything that is trying to kill you. Samson was so entrenched that he did not realize that he was in love with his enemy.

Loving two is hard to do.

You must love one and hate the other (Luke 16:13)

God said choose ye this day whom you are going to serve (Joshua 24:15).

I'm going to choose God...how about you?

Let Your NO be NO

If you learn anything from the story of Samson, learn the power of no. Learn to get out before you see the burning house. Learn to escape when you smell a stench of fire. Don't let your curiosity kill your anointing. Don't let your flesh win over your faith. Learn to say no; and mean no! The power of "no" loses it effectiveness every time you flirt with the enemy. The power of "no" loses consistency when your enemy's hear you say it, but still, they call you bluff. If you have to cry, say no. If you have to be alone, say no. If you have to move out and lose it all, say no. When you say "no," God will say yes. God will open up doors for you that you never imagined were there. God will turn your EX-, into an experience for somebody else. God will make you an overcomer, each time you say no. You may lose friends, but that's alright. Say no anyway. They might call you "holier than thou," but remember who you are. You belong in the mountain, not in the valley. You are the head and not the tail. You are above and not beneath (Deuteronomy 28:13). When you say no, keep it as a no. That way, you can make room for the blessing He has in store after you have resisted the enemy at all costs.

There is a reward for obedience. How bad do you want the reward?

CHAPTER FOUR

Get It Out Of Your System

In the spring, at the time when kings go off to war, David sent Joab out with the king's men and the whole Israelite army. They destroyed the Ammonites and besieged Rabbah. But David remained in Jerusalem. One evening David got up from his bed and walked around on the roof of the palace. From the roof he saw a woman bathing. The woman was very beautiful, and David sent someone to find out about her. The man said, "She is Bathsheba, the daughter of Eliam and the wife of Uriah the Hittite." Then David sent messengers to get her. She came to him, and he slept with her. (Now she was purifying herself from her monthly uncleanness.) Then she went back home. The woman conceived and sent word to David, saying, "I am pregnant."
2 Samuel 11:1-5

And David said unto Nathan, I have sinned against the LORD. And Nathan said unto David, The LORD also hath put away thy sin; thou shalt not die.
2 Samuel 12:13

In 2 Samuel, we discover the story of a man named David. David was a King, he was a warrior, and he was a praiser. David could have any woman he wanted. He, like Samson, had an issue with lust. He had an issue with wanting what belonged to others. He had a struggle between doing right for the Lord, and pleasing his flesh. In this instance, David chose the wrong pleasure. He decided to enjoy another man's wife, and when the prophet came to expose David, he immediately repented (after realizing that this guilty man in the prophet's parable was him), and he asked the Lord to forgive him. The Lord did forgive him, but his decisions did not come without consequences.

The story is very powerful, so I encourage you to read it in its entirety. But the reason I bring this up is because, like all of us, David could not get his EX out of his system. His EX wasn't a person; his EX was a poison. His poison was lust. His poison was unrighteous desires. His poison was imputed into him every time he slept with another woman; every time he flirted with the enemy; every time he used his power to feed his poison. Days after intercourse, the longing would continue. The desires would increase. He couldn't get it out of his system. He tried praying, he tried working, he went out on the battlefield hoping to extinguish these desires, but nothing worked. As soon as he found himself by himself, he would fall into the trap again.

> ***[David's] EX wasn't a person; his EX was a poison... lust... unrighteous desire.***

Sounds like some of you reading this book. You do very well testifying in church with a microphone in your hand. But what about when there are no witnesses, and you can afford to go on that cruise – far away from the nosey members who go to your church? What about when you pay your tithes faithfully, but you lie on your taxes so that you can get a greater return illegally? What about when you are boasting about the A's and B's you received on your report card, but you forgot to tell the time you plagiarized off of someone else's research paper because you waited until the last minute to do your work. Readers beware! You've got to be careful not to scream deliverance in public, but struggle with your poison in private. Deliverance isn't tested when the lights are on. Deliverance isn't proven when you are sitting on the front row in a conference. Deliverance is tested after you go upstairs to the hotel room—knowing a few EX's are waiting for you to send them a text message to "come on up." Don't boast until you're sure you are delivered. If you boast prematurely, you'll find yourself like David—repenting, punished, and broken.

He needed deliverance.

You need deliverance.

We all need deliverance.

But let me be honest. The problem I have with the subject of deliverance, is that many people tell you to be delivered but they don't tell you *how*. They make it seem so easy—quote a few verses, delete a few numbers, and slap some holy oil across your forehead. But they don't discuss the seasons where deliverance gets difficult to maintain. They look at you and judge you for what you did last summer, but they won't tell you what they did last week! I've got a major problem with the way people talk about deliverance.

You see, the primary reason you keep going back to your EX, is not because you don't want to leave it alone; it's because you don't know HOW to leave it alone. You don't know how to shake off this desire to go back to something that you know was never good for you in the first place. You aren't sure about your ability to say "no" (as we discussed in the previous chapter). So, you continue in this cycle of pain, pleasure, and apology.

Lord I'm sorry for doing it...
.....I'll never do it again.
.....Lord just this one time, I promise.
..... I'll do right next time.
.......Lord, why in the world did I ever go back?
This did not help me move forward at all.

And the cycle continues:

Lord I'm sorry for doing it...
.....I'll never do it again.
.....Lord just this one time, I promise.
..... I'll do right next time.
.......Lord, why in the world did I ever go back?

In this chapter, I want to give you some solid tools and tips to help you "GET IT OUT OF YOUR SYSTEM." You may not know what it's like to be a drug addict, or an alcoholic—you're probably too saved for struggles like that—but I guarantee you, some of us with whom you go to church know what it's like to be addicted to something that isn't addicted to you. We know what it's like to hear this thing calling our name, even when we've said no once and for all. When sin gets in your system, you can experience withdrawal even after you experience deliverance. Withdrawal is that process of longing. It's when you desire something that your body has decided not to indulge in. Withdrawal is that pain you feel when you stop feeding your habit with the toxins that used to keep it alive. When we discuss getting this EX out of your system, you've got to reflect over your life and remember your withdrawal season.

What made you go back?

How did it feel when you went back?

Why are you not still involved with it if it was as good as it seemed?

This is the first part of getting it out of your system. I call it "checking our history." You know how to search the history on the internet browser, so that you can trace the sites you've visited. In the same matter, we've got to check our history. We've got to stop clearing the history, but keep it there as a marker for what we will NOT do again.

When we remember what it felt like to be in bondage again, our minds will keep our feet from stumbling into that action again. Philippians 2:5 tells us "let this mind be in you which was also in Christ

Jesus." You've got to know how to direct your mind toward Christ, and not bow down to your EX.

THIS IS NOT A GAME; THIS IS WARFARE!

The second component of getting it out of your system is to recognize that you are in a spiritual battle. Any time God is about to send you into a blessed place, you can always count on a component called spiritual warfare. You can always count on opposition. If opposition isn't there, your blessing is still farther away from you than you realize. Opposition is the key to promotion. Spiritual warfare is the term we use to describe an invisible opponent, but a palpable fight going on up above our heads. The demons of darkness and the angels of light are warring for your soul. Spiritual warfare is when you go through a war in your mind. One thought says, "go" and the other thought says "no." One day you are praying, and the other day you are playing. This is spiritual warfare. It's when you have to apply the Word in order to get out, and apply prayer in order to stay out. It's when you try to fight with your physical strength, but you only come up defeated and tired. Spiritual warfare requires relationship with God. Listen: Satan is not going to allow you to get what God promised you without a struggle. In order to get out and stay out, you've got to know that Satan wants to kill you. He absolutely wants to annihilate you (John 10:10). He's not playing games. He wants your very life on a silver platter. Know that you are in spiritual warfare.

Do Not Go Anywhere where God is NOT

Know your limits and study your war zones. ***Do not go anywhere where God is not.*** That includes clubs, the hotel, the streets, and house parties. The Lord is everywhere. His presence is not. The eyes of the Lord are in every place, beholding the good and evil (Proverbs 15:3), but His spirit will not thrive with man always (Genesis 6:3). If God is nowhere around the place you are going, you just don't need to go. Blessed is the man who walks not in the counsel of the ungodly, nor stands in the way of the sinner, nor sits in the seat of the scornful (Psalm 1:1). If it's ungodly, avoid it. If the stench of sin is all over it, go the other way. If all your friends do is gossip and hate on everybody, delete them from your life. People have familiar spirits even in their homes, and in their cars. Know the environment that you need to be entertaining. We need to stay in the confines of where we know the presence of God is. The more you dwell in the safety of God's presence, the more you will be able to discern where God is and where God is not.

We need to stay in the confines of where we know the presence of God is.

Wait on the Lord

If good things come to those who wait, then bad things must come to those that rush. You've got to learn how to slow down. Wait on the Lord and listen for his direction. Often, we can't get the EX out of our system because we run to it before we wait on God. We grab our phone before we grab the Bible. God becomes an afterthought, not the first fruit!

When someone prophesies to you, the Word they are speaking over your life could come today or it could come ten years from now. Abram received the promise of a son, but it took decades for this word to come to pass. It took so long that, he and Sarah decided to make God's word come true. You can't make God move any faster than God has already planned to move. You can only delay your destiny trying to rush God along. God doesn't need your help. Slow down and wait on Him.

Don't rush through any season. There are four seasons in the year: summer, spring, fall and winter. In all seasons, the temperature fluctuates. Your clothes change according to the season you are in. There are some days of unexpected warmth even in the winter, and if you rush through the season, you won't be dressed appropriately for the outside forces. Just because you are in a particular season, doesn't mean it is the right time. Let God take His time. He knows the season and time you are in.

Maintain your Worship Life with God

Christians talk a good game, but our track record shows that we let go of God too easily. You've got to learn how to maintain your worship life with God. This is more vital than any other component. In order to get one thing out of your system, you've got to put something else in. An empty vessel only becomes open vacancy for the enemy to infiltrate and corrupt all over again. **Good upkeep enables you to keep up.** Some people are guilty of bad maintenance. If you start a routine of loving and worshipping God daily, then you won't struggle to move forward. You won't be caught off guard. Maintenance keeps you where you need to be so that God can hear you and receive your praises. In this season, God is requiring his people to uphold a standard of righteousness, holiness and commitment. If you say that you are a Christian, your life ought to prove it. Life has a way of testing us to show us what we are really made of. But commit to maintaining your worship life with God. Be who God says that you already are. Get the poison out of your system, and download purpose into your system.

Admit when YOU are Wrong

And David said unto Nathan, I have sinned against the LORD. And Nathan said unto David, The LORD also hath put away thy sin; thou shalt not die.
2 Samuel 12:13

Notice I didn't say "Admit IF you are wrong." Without a doubt, there will come a day WHEN you are wrong. No man is perfect. No woman has lived a sin free life. You must learn the power of repentance of godly sorrow action. You will never get into God's good graces until you learn how to admit that you have done wrong. If God killed us for the things that we did wrong, there would be no one in the world. So He isn't looking down from heaven waiting to destroy you. His mercy is so abundant, He wants to hear you repent so that He can extend grace toward you. When you make a decision to get it out of your system, true repentance comes naturally.

God does not celebrate the results of sin.

Howbeit, because by this deed thou hast given great occasion to the enemies of the LORD to blaspheme, the child also that is born unto thee shall surely die. 15And Nathan departed unto his house. And the LORD struck the child that Uriah's wife bare unto David, and it was very sick.
2 Samuel 12:14

When you are wrong, you are just wrong. No way to sugar coat it; no way to lie around it. Sin has taken on the form of "greater or lesser" in human eyes, but to God, sin is sin. Whether others see it or not, it doesn't matter. When we sin, we sin against God and only God. God sees it all. So the first thing that you must do is admit, "I made a mistake. I messed up." Even though David lost his son because of his sin, he did not lose his life. God does not celebrate the results of sin. God said that He would kill the child, but God does not take pleasure in penalizing us. He just could not bless their process of procreation. The same is true for us. When we birth something that He didn't intend, there will be consequences. God does not take pleasure in chastising us for the things that we have done. Nevertheless, He punishes us because He loves us.

Likewise, we shouldn't condemn ourselves for a mistake we've made and a sin we've already repented for. Some people in the church love to point fingers and shun others when they find out that others have sinned. But the Bible says that all have sinned and come short of the glory of God. Hands off. The moment you point your finger at me, there are four more fingers pointing back at you. Anytime you sin against God, know that your excuses are not the proper way to begin a conversation with God. You can't blame anyone else. You can't go to Him saying, "if I had a father, I would've done this;" or "If I had an education, I would've done this." No! This is no one else's fault but your own. Even if another person played a role in the sin, everyone must work out their own souls salvation with fear and trembling (Philippians 2:12).

Either God Kills it...or He Kills YOU

God does not allow your past to have a future. He allowed David's son which was birthed out of the will of God to die in order to avoid it happening again. Either God kills it, or He kills you. It is not helping you. It is causing you to become more broken, more dependable, and more depressed. The sin is separating you from God. So God had to destroy it before it destroyed you. *Get it out of your system.* Some people are clogged up and need a detoxification. People are too cloudy, but if you get the wrong people out of your life, the wrong things will stop happening. Although God is not pleased with you, He will allow you to struggle for a season so that you can appreciate life without the struggle. The penalty for the crime that David and Bathsheba committed was death. Even though David was a king, he still had to pay for his sin. This was the biggest mistake of his entire life. In spite of David's sin, God loved him so much that he gave him grace. Romans 5 reminds us: where sin abides, grace abides all the more.

A MISTAKE CAN BECOME A GATE!

It is possible to get better from having gone through a mistake, but if a mistake turns into continual mistakes, you have a pattern. You date the same person over and over. It's a different body and different face but the same person. You've changed people but you are still dating the same poison. Recognize the pattern. If you quit your job every three months, it is not your job's fault. It is yours. You may have an issue with commitment. It is a pattern. If you make a mistake, schedule a conference with God. Confess to God when you do something you should not have done. Schedule it quickly. Get the mess out of you. Get rid of not being able to forgive. We have to know when to hold on and when to let go. Ask for forgiveness. Forgiveness is the act of releasing a painful memory or the guilt from a past mistake/sin. God never binds us to our past, he allows us to move on from it. If you do all this, your mistake will become a gate. It will open you up to God and become a portal by which God can use your test as a testimony. If you do right by your mistake the first time, you won't get used to the pattern of perpetual sin. Turn your mistake into a gate. Repent, ask for forgiveness, and let this situation usher you into a new level of understanding others and forgiving yourself.

There is good news even for your mistake... God's mercy is still with you.

David therefore besought God for the child; and David fasted, and went in, and lay all night upon the earth. And the elders of his house arose, and went to him, to raise him up from the earth: but he would not, neither did he eat bread with them. And it came to pass on the seventh day, that the child died. And the servants of David feared to tell him that the child was dead: for they said, Behold, while the child was yet alive, we spake unto him, and he would not hearken unto our voice: how will he then vex himself, if we tell him that the child is dead?
(2 Samuel 12:16-23)

David did not eat. He probably couldn't sleep. He became depressed. When you have sinned and not confessed, you open the door for physical, spiritual and mental sickness. He stopped his worship. He hid in his guilt and shame. The servants came to him and told him that his child had died a week after it was born. Then David got up, and ate. Once he found out that it was dead, he got up from his failure and began to live again. There is good news even for your mistake. The good news is, God's mercy is still with you. Why? Because you're still alive to tell the story. According to Old Testament law, David deserved to die because of his adulterous act with someone else's wife. But God spared his life even though he took his son's life. God is protecting you even in your mess-up moments. God is covering you even when you forget about Him. That is reason enough to praise God right now. Even though it is cloudy outside, the sun is still shining. Even though there are consequences, there are also undeserved blessings that God has prepared for you. You are a winner. And you will conquer this EX-situation; in Jesus' name!

Declare this today:

I'm not what I did.

I am not who I was.

Sin will not hold me captive.

I will remove myself from this environment.

I will refresh my worship.

I will get this poison out of my system.

CHAPTER FIVE

Beware of Snaky Talk

I was once told a story about a snake who was found in the snow. It was cold outside, and the snake thought that he would freeze to death and die. A young man saw him lying still in the snow. Even though he appeared lifeless, the young man was afraid to pick him up. Why? Well, because he was a *snake*! To the young man's surprise, the snake started begging to be picked up. He said, "Please pick me up. All I need is a little warmth."

The young man said, "No! You are a snake and you bite people."

The snake continued. He could see the hesitancy in the young man's face, but he also knew that body heat would warm him. So He asked again:

"Please pick me up. I promise I will behave. I am just cold and I know I'm going to die."

The young man insisted, "No, I won't give in. You are a snake. You bite people." Well, the snake continued to beg and plead; promising not to bite him if he helped him. He did this all day until finally, against the young man's better judgment, he picked up the snake and put him under his shirt to get him warm.

The snake loved the warmth of the young man's body. He loved this new home. He felt himself returning to his normal *cold-blooded* temperature. The snake got so warm and comfortable that he remembered he was a snake and bit the young man. The young man scolded the snake badly for biting him. He reminded him of his promise and how he tried to help him.

The snake replied, "I'm sorry. I could not help myself; but you knew I was a snake when you put me in your shirt."

> ***...many times, we embrace people who look. like.. walk like snakes, and yet we call them saints.***

The name of this chapter is "Beware of Snaky Talk." I named it that because many times, we embrace people who look like snakes, walk like snakes, and yet, we call them saints. They are low-down, grimy, slithery, and deceptive. They will get you to trust them and they will play on your sympathy. They like to appeal to your compassion. And all along they don't possess the character to keep their word, nor do they mean you any good. They will bite you with words and their actions will ALWAYS inflict pain in the end.

These *snaky* traits should not come to us as a surprise. In fact, the spirit of snaky talk has been around since Genesis. Deception is at the heart of the snake's conversation. Destruction is his goal. He detects a weakness, and *talks* his way into it. He uses the way he looks and the way he talks as a way to get into a space that should have never been opened to him.

Now the serpent was more subtle than any beast of the field which the LORD God had made. And he said unto the woman, Yea, hath God said, Ye shall not eat of every tree of the garden? And the woman said unto the serpent, We may eat of the fruit of the trees of the garden: But of the fruit of the tree which is in the midst of the garden, God hath said, Ye shall not eat of it, neither shall ye touch it, lest ye die. And the serpent said unto the woman, Ye shall not surely die: For God doth know that in the day ye eat thereof, then your eyes shall be opened, and ye shall be as gods, knowing good and evil. And when the woman saw that the tree was good for food, and that it was pleasant to the eyes, and a tree to be desired to make one wise, she took of the fruit thereof, and did eat, and gave also unto her husband with her; and he did eat. And the eyes of them both were opened, and they knew that they were naked; and they sewed fig leaves together, and made themselves aprons. And they heard the voice of the LORD God walking in the garden in the cool of the day: and Adam and his wife hid themselves from the presence of the LORD God amongst the trees of the garden. And the LORD God called unto Adam, and said unto him, Where art thou? And he said, I heard thy voice in the garden, and I was afraid, because I was naked; and I hid myself. And he said, Who told thee that thou wast naked? Hast thou eaten of the tree, whereof I commanded thee that thou shouldest not eat? And the man said, The woman whom thou gavest to be with me, she gave me of the tree, and I did eat. And the LORD God said unto the woman, What is this that thou hast done? And the woman said, The serpent beguiled me, and I did eat. And the LORD God said unto the serpent, Because thou hast done this, thou art cursed above all cattle, and above every beast of the field; upon thy belly shalt thou go, and dust shalt thou eat all the days of thy life: And I will put enmity between thee and the woman, and between thy seed and her seed; it shall bruise thy head, and thou shalt bruise his heel. Unto the woman he said, I will greatly multiply thy sorrow and thy conception; in sorrow thou shalt bring forth children; and thy desire shall be to thy husband, and he shall rule over thee. And unto Adam he said, Because thou hast hearkened unto the voice of thy wife, and hast eaten of the tree, of which I commanded thee, saying, Thou shalt not eat of it: cursed is the ground for thy sake; in sorrow shalt thou eat of it all the days of thy life;

***Genesis 3:1-17** (KJV)*

As you read this text in Genesis 3, you're probably thinking, "tell me something I don't know." These folks in the Bible are popular. We think we know all there is to know about them. Adam, Eve, and the serpent are seen everywhere: in museums, in books, in music, and paintings around the world. But of these three, aside from Eve's curiosity and Adam's so-called weakness, the Serpent is most disturbing.

Be careful. The person you consider your best friend may be a snake.

By and large, people do not like snakes. They cringe at the thought of them. It is not just how they look, but how they act. Snakes are unpredictable and sneaky. With one bite they can let out poisonous venom that can paralyze the body or destroy it. The venom stops the body's normal function. It is not the external damage that causes snakes to be feared, it is what they do to the inside of you. Once something has been said, it cannot be taken back. Snaky talk can affect your emotions, delude your mind, and destroy the way you see things.

And yet, as much as people hate snakes, they don't see the snake-like people that surround them. Snakes blend in very well. They are good at camouflaging themselves. They never expose the knife behind their backs. They talk a good game, but their track records shows that they don't do anything but talk their way into your heart. Be careful. The person you consider your best friend may be a snake. Your greatest snake could be your co-worker, a supervisor, a relative, a lover, or even someone in the church. Snakes are everywhere and can be anyone. Therefore, we must be discerning of those around us. And keep your true friends close. They are the only ones who will be able to protect you from snake dangers.

EVERYTHING THAT GLITTERS...

What we see in Genesis is that Eve slips off from her covering, Adam. Adam represents her pastor. He is her husband. He is her shield. She has a conversation with the Serpent, who of course, is the Devil. But he comes to Eve in the form of a snake. This is a good point to remind ourselves that the Devil may take on many forms. These forms may be very attractive.

Look at what 2 Corinthians 11:14 says,

And no marvel; for Satan himself is transformed into an angel of light. (KJV)

Satan always has to put himself inside of a body. The outward appearance may be the perfect package designed to take you out. You know what they say: "Everything that looks good, ain't good for you," and "Everything that glitters is not gold." You need to follow those golden rules. Sometimes, when the man is too attractive, you need to ask yourself "what's wrong?" If the woman is ready to go from "how are you" to "will you marry me," you may need to step back and see if she looks like the snake. If your new business partners are all talk but they have no records of what they have accomplished, you need to kindly dismiss them with "we'll call you, don't call us." Whatever the enemy puts before us, is only to distract us from what God has for us. Everything that glitters ain't gold!

But there is something else here that is a major concern. Eve does not understand the commandment. She knows that God has said something. But she is not sure how it applies to her. For us, this is like us hearing the Word but not knowing how to apply it to our lives. Her lack of understanding opened a door for the Serpent to manipulate God's Word and trick Eve. He gets Eve to believe that God's Word is open for interpretation. He convinces her that she needs him in order to understand God.

Let me pause right there and say: there is only one mediator—Jesus Christ. Yes, God will place people in your life to help you through life's trials, but the truth is, all you need is the Holy Ghost to guide you into all truth. The moment you become addicted to a man's guidance or an international preacher's words, you become a candidate for modern day idolatry. Don't let any man convince you that you can't live without him. If God has been faithful to keep you this far, He surely won't let you down now! Don't let anybody trick you into thinking that your life is average without their "above average" personality. Eve was too naïve. She didn't realize that all she needed was her covering and her covenant with God. All you need is your covering and your covenant with God. You may not have a husband, but if you are apart of a church, stay under the covering. Don't just run here and there trying to find out what the Word of the Lord is for your life. Get down on your knees in your living room and don't get up until you hear from God for yourself!

DON'T DOUBT WHAT GOD HAS ALREADY SAID!

Because of her weakness, the serpent planted doubt in her mind about what God has said. The serpent convinced her that God was hiding something from her. He made her believe that God did not want her and Adam to become gods; which is why he stopped them from eating the fruit. His snaky talk was slick. He turned her from desiring God and made her focus on herself. Anytime someone calls themselves "speaking into your life," but the end result leads to self-confidence, self-righteousness, or an "I can do this without God" mentality, this 'word' isn't coming from the Lord. This is snaky talk!

How can someone say they love God, but they always doubt Him?

Eve was no match for the Devil. She couldn't beat him if she tried. This kind of dialogue is dangerous. Conversations that confuse you about the meaning of God's Word ruin your faith if you're not careful. The serpent wasn't a messenger from God; he was a messenger from Satan. How can someone say they love God, but they always doubt Him? His name is Faithful! God is all-knowing. God is all-powerful. What God says will come to pass. What He destroys will be destroyed. It's as simple as that: God is God!

The serpent didn't care about Eve's relationship with God. His goal was to create divorce. He wanted to drive a wedge between the Creator and creation. Mind you, he is doing all of this by talking. He is using words to enter Eve's mind and heart. The Bible describes him as "more subtle than any beast of the field which the LORD God had made." This is not a positive subtlety; this is the kind that is linked to craftiness.

You have probably heard of "crafting an argument." This means that the words spoken are meant to shape your thinking and change your opinion. In the case of Genesis 3, the serpent wanted to poison Eve against God. He was a snake, and venom was his specialty. Snakes use their venom to destroy the body. And the same is true of their human counterparts. People who act like snakes or have a snake's mentality are messy. They slither around into everybody's business. They shoot venom on top of your victory; they love to destroy what you have designed.

If they are messy, you know they are also liars and exaggerators. They hiss and gossip. They stretch and distort the truth. They are miserable people who have no life. And because they have no life, they feel that their assignment in life is to disrupt, discourage, and dismantle everyone else's life. Note: they have not always been snakes. The Bible says that the serpent crawled on his belly after the deception of Eve. They may have been alright in the beginning, but once they became envious and jealous of you, they became "snaky." Now they cannot be trusted. Now you can't leave your kids with them, and you better not leave your spouse around them unprotected. Regardless of how friendly they look, or how good they talk, you cannot trust them. They shed their skins so that they look different but the core of who they are is not changed. They only have a new skin. They will still bite you because they are still snakes.

I SURVIVED THE BITE

And when they were escaped, then they knew that the island was called Melita. And the barbarous people shewed us no little kindness: for they kindled a fire, and received us every one, because of the present rain, and because of the cold. And when Paul had gathered a bundle of sticks, and laid them on the fire, there came a viper out of the heat, and fastened on his hand. And when the barbarians saw the venomous beast hang on his hand, they said among themselves, No doubt this man is a murderer, whom, though he hath escaped the sea, yet vengeance suffereth not to live. And he shook off the beast into the fire, and felt no harm. Howbeit they looked when he should have swollen, or fallen down dead suddenly: but after they had looked a great while, and saw no harm come to him, they changed their minds, and said that he was a god. Acts 28:1-6 (KJV)

Snakebites are a snake's defense mechanism. (Proverbs 23:32) *At the last it biteth like a serpent, and stingeth like an adder.* (KJV) They intend to discourage, paralyze, and kill. This was the case in Genesis as well as the passage above. Paul is trying to help the people recover from the experience of shipwreck. He is trying to calm them from the fear of almost drowning. Paul was picking up sticks to build a fire. He wanted to help those he had been ministering to and prophesying to. He builds a fire and when it gets hot, out jumps a viper. It was lurking and waiting, all the time. Things were going according to plan until the viper jumped on Paul's hand. The Apostle Paul was headed to see Caesar. He determined not to let this bite stop him. The kind of bite he had should've caused him to die. His followers thought that this was it for Paul. He would survive the shipwreck, but not the snakebite. Interestingly enough, the text does not say that anyone tried to help him. Rather than help, they began to think about what he might have done wrong.

You should've checked into a mental ward. But look at how God has spared you!

Isn't it amazing how people always want to know what you did before they reach out a helping hand? Why do we jump to judgment all the time, thinking that God is punishing someone? What if this is an opportunity for God to show himself mighty on your behalf?

Paul couldn't let the snaky talk distract him. He had to know his calling and he had to set his eyes on the prize of destiny. Paul could only depend on God to sustain him through this situation. The Bible tells us that Paul simply shook the viper off. I love the way the text says, "He should have swollen." He should've died. In fact, there are a lot of things that "should have" happened to you. You should've had a sexually transmitted disease. You should've been broke for the rest of your life. You should've been in rehab. You should've checked into a mental ward. But look at how God has spared you! Look at how faithful God has been to you!

You survived the bites of pain, the stress, the lies, the foreclosure, the repossession, the sickness, the divorce. You survived the bite. Now, people have to change their minds about you. Tell them to keep watching. They will eventually change their minds. What the Devil meant for evil, God will turn it around for good. As God begins to turn around the trouble in your life, the snakes will have to change their minds about your God. Why? Because you survived the bite.

TAKE IT UP TO PUT IT DOWN!

And these signs shall follow them that believe; in my name shall they cast out devils; they shall speak with new tongues; they shall take up serpents; and if they drink any deadly thing, it shall not hurt them; they shall lay hands on the sick, and they shall recover.

Mark 16:17-18 (KJV)

You need to remember who you are. You need to know that God has put something unique in you. There is something special about us believers. I am not referring to our denominations or our fancy creeds. I am talking about those believers who study the Word of God to understand the promises of God. I am referring to believers who lay hold on God's promises and wait in expectation for the manifestation of it. Signs follow you. Signs follow those whose trust is in

God, and not themselves.

We are used to the idea of following signs, but here the Bible says that signs follow us. Signs are for direction. Signs are for protection. Signs create expectations. Trust me, people read signs.

There is good news even for your mistake... God's mercy is still with you.

Ever wondered why people are so attracted to your character? It's because signs FOLLOW YOU. They are reading the signs of your life. Every time God blesses you, a sign goes up. Every time you fast and pray instead of curse and fuss, a sign goes up. So our belief paints the message of victory over demonic oppression. The believer has power over the influence of the Devil. The believer has the power over every snake that tries to spit venom at us. When we begin to speak in our heavenly language, we convey to God what human words cannot utter. That which is intended to hurt us won't and can't. The devil knows this. The devil knows that he is already a defeated foe. Why? Because signs follow us. Sick people recover when we lay hands on them. People in bankrupt situations begin to flourish and succeed when we pray for them. Signs follow us.

So leave this chapter with the strength to know: the enemy is not stronger than the God in you! Yes, you will take up serpents. The thing that inspired fear in your life, you will not let the enemy haunt you for the rest of your life. The thing that was intended to kill you, it will now fear you killing it. The people who talked junk to you, will now listen to your proclamation of strength and power. That situation that once fastened itself to you will now feel you put in under your feet to be crushed by the God of peace. Take it up, to put it down. Take up your sign, and put down the enemy's design.

Be sensitive to the Spirit.
Listen to wise counsel.
Pay attention to your leader.

Ask God to anoint your ears. Ask God to touch your eyes. Don't just listen to what people say, examine the motive of their hearts. No matter what you go through, God will protect you. He cares. You are not in this alone. The good news is, the serpent's head has already been bruised by Christ. That means you win. That means he loses. Don't listen to the snake. He is a liar. He always has been and always will be.

Chapter Six

Cheaters

The word of the LORD came to me: "Son of man, confront Jerusalem with her detestable practices and say, 'This is what the Sovereign LORD says to Jerusalem: Your ancestry and birth were in the land of the Canaanites; your father was an Amorite and your mother a Hittite. On the day you were born your cord was not cut, nor were you washed with water to make you clean, nor were you rubbed with salt or wrapped in cloths. No one looked on you with pity or had compassion enough to do any of these things for you. Rather, you were thrown out into the open field, for on the day you were born you were despised.

Then I passed by and saw you kicking about in your blood, and as you lay there in your blood I said to you, "Live!" I made you grow like a plant of the field. You grew and developed and entered puberty. Your breasts had formed and your hair had grown, yet you were stark naked. Later I passed by, and when I looked at you and saw that you were old enough for love, I spread the corner of my garment over you and covered your naked body. I gave you my solemn oath and entered into a covenant with you, declares the Sovereign LORD, and you became mine.

I bathed you with water and washed the blood from you and put ointments on you. I clothed you with an embroidered dress and put sandals of fine leather on you. I dressed you in fine linen and covered you with costly garments. I adorned you with jewelry: I put bracelets on your arms and a necklace around your neck, and I put a ring on your nose, earrings on your ears and a beautiful crown on your head. So you were adorned with gold and silver; your clothes were of fine linen and costly fabric and embroidered cloth. Your food was honey, olive oil and the finest flour. You became very beautiful and rose to be a queen. And your fame spread among the nations on account of your beauty, because the splendor I had given you made your beauty perfect, declares the Sovereign LORD.

Ezekiel 16: 1-14

There is a popular syndicated reality TV show called "Cheaters." It's based out of Dallas, Texas. The entire show is all about exposing people who have cheated on their significant other. The show is popular because most people cheat, but few people are caught. So these episodes try to warn viewers about the possibility of being caught on camera! It's one thing to be exposed in private; it's an entirely different thing to be exposed in public.

The Cheaters Detective Agency begins by interviewing the person who is complaining. Usually this helpless woman is crying about her man not being home at night; she's finding suspicious phone numbers in his pants; or she sees any number of clues that lead her to conclude that she's being cheated on.

The episode begins.

The detective team finds the culprit, exposes his act on television, and the cheater has an opportunity to make his case in front of the detectives. Normally, when the cheater is caught, he is outraged. He is mad. The cheater explodes in anger, and the one who has been cheated on ends up crying and moving on. Sometimes these couples stay together, but most often, they go their separate ways.

We all are CHEATERS: Don't Judge Me!

Now I'm going to say something that might make some of the "deep" saints a little mad. Everyone may not have been cheated on, but everyone has been a cheater. All of us have cheated on God at one point in our lives. If you haven't cheated on God, and you say that you are in relationship with him, you lie. Whenever we sin, we cheat on God. David said "unto thee and thee only do I sin" (Psalm 51:4). When we mess up, we cheat on God. When we choose our EX over Him, we cheat on God. Whenever we break covenant with God to enjoy our moment of pleasure, we cheat on God. We are CHEATERS. We have cheated in the past and some of you may be cheating on God right now!

Everyone may not have been cheated on, but everyone has been a cheater.

But in order to be free from the anger you've felt when someone cheated on you, you've first got to admit, "I'm a cheater, too." You've got to stop pointing fingers and examine yourself. When did you hurt someone? When were you a stumbling block in someone else's life? When was God disappointed in you because you made all the wrong decisions? You must confess your truth, repent for your mistakes, and be free from the blame game. We are not delivered when we blame other people. We are delivered when we throw up our hands and say, "It's me Lord! It's me Lord! Standing in the need of prayer."

This chapter is called CHEATERS. I'm not writing so that you can pinpoint somebody else or accuse another for destroying your life. This chapter is about exposing the CHEATER in you. You can't change what other folks have done to you, but you can examine yourself and recognize what you have done to others. Most importantly, you need to recognize what you have done to God.

So You Want to Be a Prophet?

Ezekiel is what they call a demonstrative prophet. God used his life to demonstrate His word. Every thing he went through, God allowed him to endure it so that the children of Israel could learn a lesson through Ezekiel's prophetic call. You see, many people want to be a prophet but they are not willing to go through anything. Are you willing for God to use your life as a lesson for the world—even if it means you will suffer? Even if God strips you of your popularity? Even if you have to struggle just to make ends meet? Ezekiel was a true prophet, but be careful what you ask for. The day you say "I'm called to be a prophet or a pastor or a minister for the name of the Lord," you give up the rights to own your life. You totally give yourself away, so that God can use you!

We say we want to be a prophet, but most times, we really just want to profit. In the kingdom, in order to reign with Him, we've got to suffer with Him. You may never get paid for your preaching. You may never get a salary at a church. But regardless of what God brings you through, you've got to be who God called you to be with or without the results. Half of the people who call themselves prophet or pastor, aren't really living out the call. Half of the people who call themselves Christians aren't really serious about kingdom business. They aren't disciples of Christ. They are cheaters in church clothes. They are perpetrating. They are trying to pimp God by cheating on God's people. They aren't dedicated. Instead, they are money hungry and they don't have the right motives. We say we want to be a prophet, but make sure you're ready for everything that comes with that package.

The Desire in Your Eyes

Ezekiel decided to say yes to the Lord a long time ago. His "yes," however, came with some trying times as he continued to live. Ezekiel married a woman—we don't know her name, but one day, Ezekiel found himself loving on her more than he loved on God. He began cheating on God with his wife. It IS possible to cheat on the Blesser with the blessing. Ezekiel exalted her higher than God's commandment.

> ***Some of us would be better Christians if we were blind.***

Scripture says in Ezekiel 24:16 "Son of man, behold, I take away from thee the desire of thine eyes with a stroke." In other words, God allowed Ezekiel's wife to have a stroke because Ezekiel lost focus with his eyes. He turned away from his desire for God and began to desire his wife with his eyes.

You better be careful what you give your eyes permission to desire. Our most vulnerable gate is our eye gate. What we see, especially what men see, affects how we feel. It affects how we respond to what we feel. Some of us would be better Christians if we were blind. Why? Because when we look at things like pornography, not only do we cheat on God, but our eyes memorizes false desire. We begin fantasizing about something that isn't real. We begin looking on a woman that is not our wife. We begin stirring the pot of lust and we remove our attention away from God. The lust of the eye is so much bigger than a beautiful woman or a handsome man. When you envy your neighbors' car, or you lust after someone's job, you turn your eye toward things that do not matter. God does not take well to us cheating on Him with our eyes. The reason our EX stays alive, is because we are constantly turning to him or her with our eyes to see if they are still there. The snake used his words in the last chapter, but sometimes your EX will use anything that will distract your eye.

Ezekiel lost focus. Ezekiel lost faith. He turned God's blessing into an opportunity for idolatry. You must be careful not to turn the gift into a god. We idolize our possessions when they matter more to us than living a life that is pleasing in God's sight. We idolize our family members when we go to them before we go to God. Whether you like it or not, God is a jealous God. He doesn't take kindly to us putting others before him. And because God is jealous, He allowed this woman to experience death so that Ezekiel could understand what

God felt about the loss of relationship with the children of Israel.

Remember what I told you: Ezekiel was a demonstrative prophet. God used his life to act out his spoken decree over the people of Israel. The same way Ezekiel put his marriage over his mission, the children of Israel put their agenda above honoring God. Listen: there are no ifs, and's, or buts about it. God must be valued higher than the things you pray to Him for. God must receive more glory for being GOD than the gym you go to in order to keep your body in shape. God must receive more honor than the boss you work for; even if you work for the President of the United States. God is above our government. The government sits upon his shoulders (Isaiah 9:6)! He does not bow down to us. We must bow down to him!

When we lose focus of our relationship with God, we cheat again and again and again. We take advantage of Him. The worst thing about cheaters is when they try to have their cake and eat it too. So we'll come to worship on Sunday to get our blessing, and then we'll serve Satan every other day of the week. We're trying to get the benefits without the faithfulness. We're trying to love our wives at night, and enjoy our mistress when our wife goes out of town for the weekend. Shame on us for trying to cheat on God! Don't we know that He sees all? Don't we realize that God knows all? God knows the place where we rise and the place where we sleep. You can't escape God's sovereign eye! So don't even try.

GOD KNOWS HOW TO GET OUR ATTENTION

When God took Ezekiel's wife, he got the prophet's attention. When God took the love of his life away, Ezekiel finally understood what it was like to be God. Imagine God sitting above your every thought and move, and hearing you place Him on the list as the final "go to" thing. Imagine God trying to warn you about this person, but you continue to press ignore when He sends signs.

> ***The same God who is loving and kind, is always just and stern.***

So you don't want to listen? OK.

Well God strips your job away from you. He takes your scholarship. He allows sickness to come on your body. He allows your business to crumble to the ground. Trust me: God knows how to get our undivided attention. He knows how to make us stop and say "Lord, forgive me." God knows how to reroute our desire. He doesn't enjoy punishing us, but when we ignore Him, He'll do what He needs to do to get our attention back.

DON'T LET DEATH COME FOR GOD TO GET YOU BACK

God told Ezekiel to tell Israel that He missed them. He loved them, but they didn't love Him in return. If you've ever been a parent, you may know how difficult it is to give love to a child who doesn't even like you. If you've ever had to sacrifice your check for someone else's wellbeing, you know how hard it is to NEVER hear them say thank you. This is what God feels like when we don't praise him. This is how God responds when we only go to Him after we lose something or need a couple of dollars. God promised to protect Israel, but when they began to cheat on Him time after time, He threatened to kill them. The same God who is loving and kind, is always just and stern. He instructed Ezekiel to warn them by saying, "if you don't turn your affection back to me, I will destroy you." Ezekiel knew by this point that God wasn't playing. How? Because he destroyed his wife with a stroke. He went through his own cheater's experience. His wife suffered because he did not put God first. She died when he woke up. The Lord spoke to Ezekiel and told him that He had lost his wife. And it wasn't because the wife did anything wrong. It was because Ezekiel had lost focus.

You must realize the big picture. You need to recognize the people to whom your life is attached. People are either blessed or cursed because of the decisions you make. People will succeed or fail because of the decisions you make. The longer you stay attached to your EX, the longer these people will live without hope. Your deliverance will help save others. Your "no" will give other people an opportunity to say "yes." When you get delivered from a "cheater's mentality," you realize that the world is bigger than you. You are not the owner of your decisions. God uses you, and God helps you so that you can help others. Ask yourself this:

How many people will die if I continue to cheat on God?

How many souls could I win if I really became sold out for Christ?

When God calls us to do something, we need to think about how it is going to affect everyone else. This woman was destroyed because of Ezekiel. When she died, the Lord told Ezekiel that he couldn't even mourn her loss. Consider the text:

Ezekiel 24:16 "Son of man, with one blow I am about to take away from you the delight of your eyes. Yet do not lament or weep or shed any tears.
Ezekiel 24:17 Groan quietly; do not mourn for the dead. Keep your turban fastened and your sandals on your feet; do not cover the lower part of your face or eat the customary food [of mourners]."
Ezekiel 24:18 So I spoke to the people in the morning, and in the evening my wife died. The next morning I did as I had been commanded.

His wife died one night, and in the morning, he had to do what God told him to do. Are you really ready to obey God? Are you ready to abandon yourself so that God can get the glory out of your life? Ezekiel made a decision not to let his past have a future. He didn't let his desire for his wife get in the way of his relationship with God. After he realized his first mistake, he didn't become a repeat offender. All of this happened in order to bring the people to a place of deliverance. God wanted Ezekiel to show them what it felt like to be 'God' for a moment. He wanted this prophet to experience the pain He felt when He lost His bride to the affections of this world.

The EX wants the Attention that Belongs to God

God is a jealous God -- not for the things that you have but for your attention. God could care less about how many jobs you have or how much money you obtain. Just make sure you give Him his attention. God loves to bless us with more. He desires that we prosper even as our soul prospers. But one thing He is not OK with, is when we rob Him of quality time with Him. Be careful when things take your attention away from God.

> ***Make sure the agenda of your life can be changed for Him.***

We have allowed things to keep us distracted from Him. Make sure the agenda of your life can be changed for Him. At any second, make sure that you are ready for God to say "go." God is looking for a praiser who will move when He says move. He is looking for a church that will respond when He says respond. He won't share His glory with our excuses. He won't share His glory with our EX's. God wants to maintain his role as the number 1 priority of our lives. And our EX, wants nothing more than to steal that attention which belongs to God. Our EX, even if they don't realize it, is opposing God whenever they say, "don't go to church today. They will be OK without you." Our EX is being used by the enemy when they say, "don't pray right now. I don't feel like hearing all of that noise." Our EX wants the attention that belongs to God. Every time we pay our beautician the tithe that belongs to God, we cheat on God. We give our EX the attention that belongs to God.

Every time we give more love to strangers than we do our own family members, we give our EX the attention that belongs to those things that God ordained in our lives. Examine where you give your attention to:

> *Is your EX in competition with God? If so, who is winning?*
> *Does God have to strip something from you to get YOU back?*
> *Why can't you let go of feeding the EX, but you can let Go of worshipping God?*

If you continue reading the story of Ezekiel, you'll see that God told the prophet not to cry over his wife. He told him to sigh within, suck it up and keep going. God used the prophet to effectively portray what it felt like to lose a bride. The people of Israel stood as a symbol of God's "wife." The church is his bride. We have given ourselves to him, and not another. So all of our attention should be focused on beautifying God; worshipping him; and keeping Him as a priority. If you want to be free from the cheater mentality, see the cheater in you first. Repent for turning your heart away from God. Ask Him to restore you before he removes the things that matter most to you.

CHAPTER SEVEN

Indecent Proposal

Then Jesus was led by the Spirit into the wilderness to be tempted by the devil. After fasting forty days and forty nights, he was hungry. The tempter came to him and said, "If you are the Son of God, tell these stones to become bread."

Jesus answered, "It is written: 'Man shall not live on bread alone, but on every word that comes from the mouth of God.'" Then the devil took him to the holy city and had him stand on the highest point of the temple. "If you are the Son of God," he said, "throw yourself down. For it is written: "'He will command his angels concerning you, and they will lift you up in their hands, so that you will not strike your foot against a stone.'"

Jesus answered him, "It is also written: 'Do not put the Lord your God to the test.' Again, the devil took him to a very high mountain and showed him all the kingdoms of the world and their splendor. "All this I will give you," he said, "if you will bow down and worship me." Jesus said to him, "Away from me, Satan! For it is written: 'Worship the Lord your God, and serve him only.'" Then the devil left him, and angels came and attended him.

Matthew 4:1-11

You've been on this EX-journey with me for six chapters, but now, in this chapter, it's time to go deeper. It's time to get to the root of our truth. For that reason, let me warn you now. Spiritual discretion is advised. No one should read the content of these next chapters unless they have experienced or know someone who has had a few indecent proposals since they've been saved. I'm not talking about when you were out in the world. I'm not talking about what you did behind the trees as a child when no one was looking. I'm talking about since you've been saved. Since you gave your life to the Lord, put on your white baptism clothes, and spoke in tongues for the first time. If you are honest enough to admit, "Yes, I've participated in, and sometimes coordinated a few indecent proposals," then you are the reader I'm writing to right now.

A lot of people are still bound and blaming the devil for something they created themselves.

I want to talk about temptation, but i need to present it from a whole new perspective. A lot of people are still bound and blaming the devil for something they created themselves. They don't like to confront the truth about their inward desires. They think that some evil force has just thrust them into evil deeds, but that is a lie from the pit of hell. Most times, temptation begins with us. When we give in, it also ends with us.

We see it.

We like it.

We take it.

And we worry about the consequences after we've participated in it.

Temptation is an indecent proposal. It flaunts something that it can't maintain. It's a quick fix. It's a fantasy or a twisted version of the truth. Temptation happens to us all, but few of us admit when we fall.

So let me go ahead and be the first partaker of confession. Maybe my truthful statement will help free you. This is my personal and true statement: I, Demarcus Pierson, promise to tell the whole truth and nothing but the truth...so help me God. I, Demarcus Pierson, have had some indecent proposals. Since I have been saved, I've had some indecent proposals. Since I have been preaching, I have had some indecent proposals. Since I have been pastoring, I have had some indecent proposals. I've entertained a few things that the devil threw my way because they looked good on the outside but they were rotten on the inside. I have given attention to things my spirit wanted to deny. I've seen myself caught in a rock and a hard place—wanting to do God's will but also wanting to please my own flesh. As a matter of fact, I have had to deal with temptation all of my life. That's part one of this confession.

Part two is more difficult to admit. But here it goes: on some of those occasions, I have and did fall. I allowed myself to accept a few of those indecent proposals. I have let my humanness interrupt my holiness. I always wanted to please God, but temptation would get in the way and ruin my focus. This is my truth, this is my testimony, and this is my story...so help me God.

I told a little of that confession because I need to kill this misconception for those reading this book who are newly saved. Even those who have been trying to live a holy life all of their lives, let me free you: just because you are saved now does not mean that you will outgrow temptation. Temptation will creep up on you at the most unexpected time, and you will find yourself in a compromising situation before you know it. Temptation will always try to outrun you. It will always try to blindside you. The end result of temptation is to trick you for a moment so that you can forfeit your future. Temptation has a goal: destroy the believer at any cost (especially when you are chosen), but you cannot keep beating yourself for going through this kind of opposition. This stuff comes with the territory!

> ***You are where you are because of the choices you've made.***

Temptation is a CHOICE

The reality is, nobody can make you do anything. God can *influence* you to do something, Satan can present situations that cause you to fall, but temptation isn't a forced thing; temptation is a choice. You either choose to do right or you can choose to do wrong. You are NOT hypnotized into sin; you make a decision to avoid the exit sign OR you give in to what your flesh desires to do. Let me free you from the excuse that, "The devil made me do it." If God can't MAKE you come to church on time, the devil can't MAKE you go to the club. If God can't MAKE you get on your knees and pray, then the devil can't MAKE you pick up an alcoholic beverage and drink it. You are in charge of your car. There aren't spirits pressing on the gas as you head down the wrong road with the wrong person at the wrong time. Temptation is a choice. Choose ye this day how you will respond when temptation knocks on your door.

Everything is a choice. Unless you live in a third world country and you are being enslaved by some horrible slavemaster, you have a choice to get up out of the bed or stay asleep and lose your job. You have a choice to be successful or to procrastinate for the rest of your life. That's why no one should get jealous of people who have attained some level of success. Why? Because I am where I am based on the choices I've made. You are where you are because of the choices you've made. You received an offer. You decided to take the offer or reject it until a better one came your way. That's life. But how you pass the test or handle temptation will determine if your choice led you to make a good decision or a disastrous one.

THERE'S A PATTERN TO TEMPTATION

Everything has a pattern. You wake up today; pray; get dressed; drive to work; eat lunch; finish work; drive home; go to church; eat dinner; go to bed, and you develop a routine of this every day. If you're a student, you know that poor study patterns will ruin your GPA, and it may even get in the way of graduating. The patterns we allow ourselves to memorize will affect our success one-way or the other. In the same way, all temptations follow the same pattern. Temptations wake up with a mission in mind, and they set out to accomplish that goal. All temptations have an end result: to steer you out of the will of God. They celebrate when we deviate. But of course, the temptation isn't going to be obvious to you in the beginning.

Satan first identifies and locates a desire inside of you. You may desire to be valued. Another may desire to be loved. You may desire to feel pleasure or to escape from the reality of pain you're experiencing right now. Another may desire validation and affection. Whatever your desire is, the enemy will begin by telling you how much you deserve it. *You deserve to be happy. You deserve to be loved. You deserve to have as much money as you want. You deserve to be the object of someone's affection.* The problem is, if you get what you deserve through illegal or sinful means, your desire has led you directly into the trap of temptation.

Many of us think that temptation is some outside force that comes over us (like a ghost) to distract us. But the truth is, temptation begins within us. It's in the Word of God. Read it for yourself:

For from within, out of a man's heart, come evil thoughts, sexual immorality, theft, murder, adultery, greed, wickedness, deceit, eagerness for lustful pleasure, envy, slander, pride, and foolishness; all of these vile things come from within.
(Mark 7:21, 22)

Paul asked a question: "Who can save me from this body of death" (Romans 7:24). James came along and confirmed this question when he wrote, "There is a whole army of evil desires at war within you" (James 4:1). These writers knew something that we have tried to dismiss for decades: evil desires come from within. It's a part of our sinful nature. It's a part of the flesh. Paul knew that his body was defiled, which is why he told us to crucify the flesh on a daily basis. James knew that we would have an unending war within us, so he told us to work our faith so that we would not be overtaken by the evil one. This "stuff" lurks within us. The temptations we experience start with a thought planted in our mind. When you keep toying around with that thought, you eventually find yourself acting on it. You eventually find yourself doing it more. You eventually begin pulling other people into it. Why? Because misery loves company. And temptation loves a team of evildoers!

Learn how to take sound counsel or you will find yourself attached to your EX.

Somebody needs to tell you the truth: temptation is the devil's toy that keeps you in pre-school. It's time to grow up! Stop letting the devil whisper lies to you. When someone confronts you and tells you the truth, learn to thank God for sending a messenger to save your life. Too many of us think, "they don't want me to be happy. They are jealous of what I've got." No! We don't want you to be stupid. We don't want you to destroy your life. Learn how to take sound counsel or you will find yourself attached to your EX. Your EX will tattoo its curse on the skin of your future, and you will never be able to separate yourself from the pain and memory of a past mistake.

It's NOT a Sin to Think

I'll tell you something: I thank God that we won't go to HELL for thinking. I thank God that He saw fit to die for my thoughts and desires, even before I acted them out. It's not a sin to think. It's a sin to act on what we think about. The key is, you've got to replace your tempting thoughts with holy thoughts. Think on lovely things; think on peacable thing. That's what scripture tells us to do.

Finally, brothers, whatever is true, whatever is noble, whatever is right, whatever is pure, whatever is lovely, whatever is admirable--if anything is excellent or praiseworthy--think about such things.
Philippians 4:8

Thinking takes work. Temptation is easier to give into when we don't think. You remember being young and immature. A lot of us wouldn't have made the silly mistakes we made if we knew how to think. We know how to use our brain, but we don't know how to think. If we can't remember what we went through the last time we got high, or the last time we got drunk, or the last time we got locked up, then we're not thinking. How do I know? Because we look up one day, and we're back on the corner again; we're back at the bar again; we're back in the courtroom again!

Think on these things. Say goodbye to one way of thinking and say hello to a new way of thinking. I'll say it this way: We must dismiss and replace; dismiss and replace. I dismiss the thought of lust and replace it with the thought of love. I dismiss the thought of stealing and replace it with the thought of earning a salary. I dismiss the thought of cheating and replace it with the thought of commitment. Replace what you dismiss. If you don't, you will leave an opening for the enemy to enter in that empty space. You will leave a gap for him to fill. You leave room for the Evil one to take residence. Dismiss and replace. That's a practical key to unlock your deliverance from temptation.

SATAN IS A MANIPULATOR

The next thing you must know is who your opponent is. Nobody gets in the boxing ring without studying his opponent. No football team will play against a team that they haven't studied their strategies and plays. It's just foolish to compete against someone you don't know or haven't done research on. You must know your spiritual opponent.

Satan is a mass deceiver and manipulator. Because he is twisted himself, he is always twisting the truth and giving half-truth. Remember I told you, if it looked like temptation, you wouldn't be tricked into it. If it walked like a duck and quacked like a duck, then chances are, you thought it was a duck...until you noticed that this duck had wings and didn't gravitate to water. You've got to be careful.

You know what twisted truth is. It's half of the story.

Be self-controlled and alert. Your enemy the devil prowls around like a roaring lion looking for someone to devour.
1 Peter 5:8

Satan is a liar, but his lies have been laced with a small ounce of truth. Satan speaks twisted truth, so you've got to be really careful. There is a small part of his trickery that sounds like it's the right thing. There's a small part of his lie that sounds like the real deal. Satan is a clever something. He will pull you in by the appearance of a fact, only to end up false at the end of the day.

Don't act like you don't know *how* to twist the truth. You remember staying out past curfew. You remember the excuses you would conjure up before coming home. Mama would ask you where you were, or why it took you so long to come back from the store. And when you answered, you told *some* of the truth—there was traffic—but you didn't tell them that you stopped by Ray-Ray's house to meet up with your play-play girlfriend. You didn't tell them that you went across town to get into some mischief before coming home. You know what twisted truth is. It's half of the story. It's a half-baked cake of truth. It's really a lie, but it has sprinkles of truth on top. You know, it's like the stuff members try to tell their pastors, thinking the pastor won't discern the real deal. *Pastor, we are not sleeping together; he's just sleeping on the couch until he can get a job. Or, Pastor I didn't know I had to tithe off of every check I received. I thought God would let me tithe every other Sunday, or every other month. Or pastor, I'm not starting my own ministry. I just want to have bible study in my living room for the people who can't come to church all the way out there!* But, you want to have bible study on the same night that your church does, and you think that's alright? Shame on you!

Oh trust me, I know twisted truth when I see it; but do you? Can you see when the devil is serving you half-truth? If you could recognize it as easily as you think, you would not be in the situation you are in right now.

YOU ARE CHOSEN!

I often hear people saying things like: *Why can't I do this one little thing and get away with it? "So and So" did it and nothing happened. That church had it and nobody knew it. So why can't I do it? Why can't we enjoy ourselves while we still have time?* And to that I have one answer: YOU'RE CHOSEN. You can't do what others do because you are chosen. You can't mess up and not get caught because the value of your gifting is greater than the mediocrity of others' wasted life.

The rules of engagement are different for you. Many are called but few are chosen. If you are chosen, choices do matter. When you are chosen, your decisions affect not just you, but the lives attached to you. When Jesus came down from fasting, he had to first recognize who He was. He wasn't just any man. He was the Christ. He was chosen by God to come down and save his people from their sins. Every decision mattered. Every place He went, mattered. The problem is, you don't know your value. You continue to live as if you are just any ole body, when God has deposited so much anointing in you. You are living beneath your means! You are accepting an indecent proposal because you don't know your worth.

You must rise up and live the way chosen people live. I know it can be boring sometimes when you see everyone else going out to parties on the weekends. But chosen people know that they have to stay in school and study, or else their entire destiny will be damaged. I know your spouse may be pretending that you don't exist. But you are chosen. Don't let his ineptitude give you a reason to be unfaithful. Stay strong! Hold your ground. Resist the temptation to leave him. You are chosen. You don't know what staying may do for him. It may save his life. It may convert his soul.

Every decision Jesus made came with a consequence. Our lives were on the line. Our souls were at stake. So Jesus didn't give into temptation because He knew that his life was chosen to help others.

The moment you will be free from the pressure of the enemy is when you realize that your life is a gift for someone else's freedom. Because of you, others will know Christ. Because of your walk, the kingdom will multiply. Because of your decisions, someone will be restored.

Listen: when the devil tempts you, or when he makes you an offer that you find hard to resist, you need to take it as a compliment. I know it was an indecent proposal, but the truth is, he wouldn't propose if he was already engaged to you. There would be no need for the devil to seek you out if you were already married to him. Take it as a compliment. Satan wants you but he can't have you. Why? Because you've already made a holy covenant with the Lord. Your goods have already been sold to the highest bidder—Jesus Christ. Who you are is a chosen vessel for God's purpose; you are not on sale; you are not for sale; and you cannot be sold.

Who you are is a chosen vessel for God's purpose; and you cannot be sold.

Satan wouldn't tempt those whom he already has. Take it as a compliment. The next time you see temptation walking by, look over your shoulder and say "thank you but no thank you." Walk away with your head held high. Something about you attracts people toward you. Something about you infuriates the enemy so much that he wants nothing more than to see you fall. Every time you say no, Satan loses sleep. He's trying to figure out the next strategy to get you to fall. But every time you say no, you build momentum to resist him the next time. You build strength in God to fight and withstand the wiles of the enemy. When you get weak, God's strength becomes perfect. He will raise up a standard against the enemy (Isaiah 59:19).

That is why we praise God! We don't praise God because we have it all together. We praise God because, when we gave in to the indecent proposal, God didn't divorce us! God didn't abandon us! Instead, he stretched his hands again and said, "Come unto me all ye that labor and I will give you rest. Take my yoke upon you and learn of me; for I am meek and lowly in heart and ye shall find rest unto your souls. For my yoke is easy and my burden is light" (Matthew 11:28-30)

What a mighty God we serve! We serve a God who sits high and looks low. We serve a God who will give his very last so that we will have the first. We serve a God who will resist temptation, even after fasting for 40 days and 40 nights, so that we would have a perfect example and no excuse. We can do it. We can resist temptation. If Jesus did it, so can I! If my Savior resisted for me, the least I can do is return the favor.

Why?

Because I'm chosen.

I'm chosen to endure temptation. I'm chosen to run this race with joy. I'm chosen to be all who God has made me to be. I'm chosen to resist the enemy so that in the end, he will flee and God will be exalted. Reader, friend, neighbor, and fellow soldier in the army of the Lord, YOU ARE CHOSEN! Don't let the indecent proposal convince you otherwise!

CHOSEN FOR THE WILDERNESS

Would you still shout if I told you that God *chose* you to endure the wilderness? Would God still be a good God if you knew He was going to strip some things away in order to sanctify you? Jesus, in this chapter, teaches us that every chosen vessel will go through a season called THE WILDERNESS. You know you are headed toward success when you experience the wilderness season. In the wilderness, your faith is tested. In the wilderness, your agility is proven. In the wilderness, you don't have props. You don't have mommy or daddy to call. You don't have your sidepiece or your pimp daddy to help you out. In the wilderness, it's just you and God. God will pull you away from the crowd sometimes just so that He can talk to you on a one-on-one basis.

So what if I told you God chose you to endure the wilderness season? You know you are in the wilderness when the EX you want to give into temptation with, won't answer the phone. When the job opportunity you wanted disappears on the day you finally decide to apply. You know you are in the wilderness when the life-lines you used to depend on to stay afloat, are now too busy to call you back. Don't get mad at them! God has removed your comfort zone so that He can strengthen your faith.

The good news is, it's only a season. Jesus knew that He was growing in grace and strength because the devil came with tempting offers. These were new things; shiny things; things that Jesus really could enjoy at the moment that the devil showed up. Listen: the devil isn't going to bring something your way that you don't want. Why would he waste his time and your time? He's only going to flatter you with something strong enough to maneuver your faith. So imagine Jesus. Weak. Worn. Tired. Hungry. And here comes the devil. The offers he makes aren't really hard tests. Jesus had the power to turn the bread into stones if He wanted to, but He still resisted. Some of us give in because it's easy; because it's free; because nobody will ever find out. So we make an excuse around why we did it because it makes sense to us in our minds. We had the power to do it. God gave us that power, so we say, "if God didn't want me to do it, He wouldn't have given me the money or the influence or the free will to make it happen." But what if I told you it was God's will for you to be hungry? What if I told you God gave you the power, but the power was not meant for you to pimp it or misuse it?

In this scripture, it was not God's will for him to eat yet. It was certainly not God's will for Jesus to eat at the command of Satan. God's will was for him to be hungry. It may have been God's will for you to be on welfare; not sell your body and sell drugs just so you could get off of government dependence. It was not God's will for you to use your anointing to misuse people's finances. It may have been God's will not to raise any money that night. You've got to learn how to test the spirit within you. What if God says, "I want you to be hungry?" What if he doesn't want you to profit at all from the CD you record? What if he is testing your trust by telling you to move out of the 5-bedroom house and into an apartment that is so small, you have to walk out in the hallway just to think?

What if?

How bad do you want to grow in this season of wilderness? Jesus was willing to obey, by any means necessary. Jesus did what we should do when we find ourselves face to face with an indecent proposal. Jesus responded with "it is written." Whenever Satan offered one thing, Jesus had a counter attack. You need to do the same. Respond with "I'm the head and not the tail." When Satan throws his darts, counterattack with "no weapon formed against me shall prosper." What is your counterattack against the enemy!? It's the Word of God. We don't wrestle against flesh and blood. We wrestle against principalities and rulers of darkness! This is what the Bible says:

Jesus had the power to turn the bread into stones if He wanted to, but He still resisted.

For we wrestle not against flesh and blood, but against principalities, against powers, against the rules of the darkness of this world, against spiritual wickedness in high places.
Ephesians 6:12

If you knew how many wicked spirits are fighting to keep you stuck to your past, you would break free now and leave every indecent proposal alone. The evil desires may come from within, but God has given us the power to tread on the serpents and scorpions, even the ones that tempt us from within (Luke 10:19). Use your power. Use your anointed power. Use your resisting power to say no to indecent proposals. Use your praying power to stay out of hazardous territory. Use your staying power to resist the enemy and run after God. Not because you want to be perfect; but do it because YOU ARE CHOSEN!

CHAPTER EIGHT

My SETBACK is a SETUP for my COMEBACK

An old legend tells the story that Satan was going to get rid of his tools. He set up an auction and lined up his tools. Envy, deceit, malice, sensuality, enmity and many other tools were to be sold to the highest bidder. One tool was priced very high. One of the bidders asked Satan, "Why do you want so much for this?" Satan replied, "This tool has always been my most useful one. It has more wear than the rest. It is used as a wedge to get into a man's mind when all other means have failed. I have used this on every person on the earth. Few knew that I was the one that was using it." No one could afford the price that Satan demanded for the tool of discouragement, so he still uses it.

...I need to burst your sanctified bubble.

I begin this chapter with this story because I need to burst your sanctified bubble. I don't want you to read this book and think that you will never have a rainy day. I don't want you to think that, "Now that I know the traps to avoid, I will never fall victim to the enemy's deception again!" No! No! No! I want you to know the whole truth. I want you to know that with God all things are possible. At the same time, I want you to be prepared for those times when you will experience a setback.

We all have them.

We all will fall.

We all will fail.

Notice I didn't say, "we all may fall or we all may fail." I didn't say that because, the truth is, we all are human. Therefore, setbacks are an inevitable part of our make up. It comes with the territory. But the good news is, if you have the Holy Ghost within you, you will feel bad about falling. You will sense the spirit of conviction telling you, "that's not right." None of us wants to disappoint God. But when we do fall, many preachers leave us to figure out how to get back up on our own two feet by ourselves. I want to help you out a little. I want to forecast hope in your future and a brighter day than your yesterday. Discouragement is not a game. You can become so discouraged about the mistake you made that you decide to mute your ministry and pause your purpose. Instead of rising again, you decide to do nothing. Instead of asking God to forgive you, you make matters worse and give your EX a permanent parking space in your life.

You begin to think that God is so upset with you that you give up all hope and throw in the towel. But, don't give up the fight yet. God knew you would fall. He made provision for every fall we would experience, before we got saved and after. There is nothing that we could ever do that would catch God by surprise. *Just think.* He knew we would mess up and He still chose us. He knew we would be addicted to this or that, and yet, He still chose us. He knew this EX would be our greatest thorn, and yet, He STILL chose us. God made provision for your setback. God put a spare tire in the trunk of your car because He knew you would get a flat tire one day. Now it's time for you to change your perception. You've got to change the way you see life and the outcomes thereof. Every setback is a setup for a comeback.

NO Person is Exempt from Set Backs

It is so important that we understand that no person is exempt from set backs. The moment you think you don't go through situations that others go through, you will become self-righteous and judgmental. That's why it doesn't matter how long you've been saved. It doesn't matter how many scriptures you can quote. You can be the greatest preacher in the world or you may prophecy addresses and social security numbers; and still, you are not exempt from a set back. They are going to happen. Just look around at our popular preachers today. Many of them have had to deal with their setback publicly. Just thank God that you were able to go through your setbacks privately. The only difference between us and them is that nobody found out. Nobody knew what you did behind the pew. Nobody saw your text message or phone log. Thousands of people aren't talking about you because God has protected you by covering your faults. But don't get it twisted. You are no better than anyone. You are no more righteous than the girl who got pregnant and now she has to suffer through the whispers as she walks to her car after church. If they knew how many times you came to church with a hangover, it may have been more obvious. If they knew your struggle with pornography, then they would be talking about you, too. Don't put your mouth on somebody else's situation. If you do, God will expose your setback in order to humble your self-righteous pride.

Don't put your mouth on somebody else's situation.

Setbacks are synonymous with cutbacks. If you have ever worked for Corporate America, you know that there may come a day (especially during the recession season) that your boss will come to your office and announce cutbacks. They'll tell you that they have to lay some folks off because the company is in danger of bankruptcy. They'll evaluate your work ethic and decide, based on longevity or productivity, if you will stay or go. But the truth is, most cutbacks are random. You have no real control over when the cutback will occur. You don't even control the decision-making process. The same is true with our spiritual setbacks. We have little control over them. They will lay us off duty without our permission. They will stop our promotion in God, and most of all, real setbacks will interfere with our increase. Our money is affected because our mind is distracted. Our future is compromised because we look up and realize that we are right back where we began. Set backs will try to cut your purpose and deter you from destiny. But if you know who is responsible for them, you won't bury your destiny in the soil of guilt and sadness.

Satan is responsible for SETBACKS

It is Satan who is in charge of a setback. He enjoys delaying our arrival. He likes to see your flight delayed. Jesus told Peter, "Satan has desired to have you, and sift you as wheat. But I prayed that your faith fail not." Remember in previous chapters, I told you that temptation was a choice. I shared with you that some things come from within, and the devil isn't always responsible for the choices we make. But, setbacks are a different species. Satan causes the setback. He wants nothing more than to sift you as wheat. He wants to shake your foundation until you throw in the towel. He smiles when you say, "I give up." He grins when you decide not to go to church. He loves it when you resign yourself and you say, "I can't take it anymore." He desires to sift you, so he begins with a setback. He begins with a familiar spirit. He starts with a situation/distraction that he knows will cause you to double-take on your way to church. He will influence a "blast from the past" to text your phone as you pull up in the parking lot of the church before bible study. He will allow your children get you to the point of anger. He will provoke them to argue with you until you want to strangle them. He knows what will make our alarm go off. So he studies our history of sin. He locates a good setback distraction and he goes in for the kill.

The Demon of Discouragement

Let me return to the subject of discouragement. I believe I need to deal with this issue more specifically because it has become the thing that brings perpetual damage to the body of Christ. Listen: setbacks will cause the believer to fall down. Falling is unavoidable. Scripture reminds us in Proverbs 24:16 that a just man falleth seven times... But the most important part of that verse is, "and riseth up again." I'm not concerned about your fall. I'm actually concerned about your rising up again. I want to know if you will let your fall determine your future or will you see it as a temporary setback. How will you respond? Will you fall and get stuck in the cement of a bad decision? Or will you get up, repent, and move forward. The moment you fall and stay down, you let disappointment set in. It's like a perm that stays in your hair too long--it will burn away new growth and destroy your outlook on life. Discouragement will memorize your pain and inflict suicidal thoughts. The demon of discouragement will bring his cousin, depression, to the party. It will cloud your hope and ruin your race. You've got to have the confidence

You've got to have the confidence in God's word in order to get out of the pit of your past.

in God's word in order to get out of the pit of your past. Trust in the Lord with all of your heart and don't lean on your own understanding. If you could've figured it out, you would not have needed God. Our setbacks remind us of how much we need the Lord to survive.

Change your perception

Discouragement will destroy you (if you let it). It's like the student who got rejected from one college and they allowed discouragement to keep them from applying ever again. It's like the mother who experienced one bad, abusive relationship. She leaves one man and now hates all men. Discouragement will veil your eyes and blind you from the truth. One bad preacher doesn't make every preacher bad. One person who didn't see your gift doesn't mean you aren't gifted. They may have been hating on you. They may have been jealous of you. They may have wanted to see you fail. But you can't let people determine your altitude in God. You've got to remember the Word of God: the steps of a good man are ordered by the Lord, and he delighteth in his ways. God is not shocked that you fell. God is only disappointed when you make your fall, final. When you place a period where God has put a comma, that is when God is most disappointed. He has ordered your steps—even your missteps. God isn't surprised by our fall. We are. So don't let the demon of discouragement keep you in a place that you're not supposed to be in.

Discouragement Strikes after VICTORY!

You know, I've studied discouragement for a long time. I realize that the demon of discouragement comes in right after a great victory. After victory, our emotions are very high. We are vulnerable and excited. And right at the time we least expect it, discouragement sets in. It happened to Elijah in 1 Kings 19:

Now Ahab told Jezebel everything Elijah had done and how he had killed all the prophets with the sword. So Jezebel sent a messenger to Elijah to say, "May the gods deal with me, be it ever so severely, if by this time tomorrow I do not make your life like that of one of them. Elijah was afraid and ran for his life. When he came to Beersheba in Judah, he left his servant there, while he himself went a day's journey into the wilderness. He came to a broom bush, sat down under it and prayed that he might die. "I have had enough, LORD," he said. "Take my life; I am no better than my ancestors."

Then he lay down under the bush and fell asleep. All at once an angel touched him and said, "Get up and eat." He looked around, and there by his head was some bread baked over hot coals, and a jar of water. He ate and drank and then lay down again. The angel of the LORD came back a second time and touched him and said, "Get up and eat, for the journey is too much for you." So he got up and ate and drank. Strengthened by that food, he traveled forty days and forty nights until he reached Horeb, the mountain of God. There he went into a cave and spent the night.

And the word of the LORD came to him: "What are you doing here, Elijah?" He replied, "I have been very zealous for the LORD God Almighty. The Israelites have rejected your covenant, torn down your altars, and put your prophets to death with the sword. I am the only one left, and now they are trying to kill me too. The LORD said, "Go out and stand on the mountain in the presence of the LORD, for the LORD is about to pass by." Then a great and powerful wind tore the mountains apart and shattered the rocks before the LORD, but the LORD was not in the wind. After the wind there was an earthquake, but the LORD was not in the earthquake. After the earthquake came a fire, but the LORD was not in the fire. And after the fire came a gentle whisper. When Elijah heard it, he pulled his cloak over his face and went out and stood at the mouth of the cave.

Then a voice said to him, "What are you doing here, Elijah?" He replied, "I have been very zealous for the LORD God Almighty. The Israelites have rejected your covenant, torn down your altars, and put your prophets to death with the sword. I am the only one left, and now they are trying to kill me too." The LORD said to him, "Go back the way you came, and go to the Desert of Damascus. When you get there, anoint Hazael king over Aram. Also, anoint Jehu son of Nimshi king over Israel, and anoint Elisha son of Shaphat from Abel Meholah to succeed you as prophet. Jehu will put to death any who escape the sword of Hazael, and Elisha will put to death any who escape the sword of Jehu. Yet I reserve seven thousand in Israel—all whose knees have not bowed down to Baal and whose mouths have not kissed him."

So Elijah went from there and found Elisha son of Shaphat. He was plowing with twelve yoke of oxen, and he himself was driving the twelfth pair. Elijah went up to him and threw his cloak around him.

There are layers of revelation in this passage. All of them speak to the demon of discouragement. First, the enemy knows that we are the weakest when we are alone. So he waits until we find ourselves alone in order to bring discouragement. In this text, Elijah had been obeying the voice of the Lord. But one negative threat caused him to run from his assignment and fear.

Don't let Jezebel kick you out of the place God has called you to be!

When people rise up against you, most of the time, they are only strong talkers—they aren't strong walkers. They can talk the talk but they can't walk the walk. If you let the distraction discourage you, the demon has won. The devil has gotten the victory out of your setback. Even if you have to get away and recollect yourself, don't let discouragement destroy your destiny decisions.

God appeared Elijah and told him to eat. Why? Because the prophet had become weak from running toward the cave. Once again we see the enemy coming at us when we are physically handicapped. When we are hungry, we don't think right. We need nourishment in order to re-focus and do what God has called us to do. So God tells him to eat. Then He shows Him that He is with Elijah. You have got to remember that God has not left you. He has not forsaken you. The demon of discouragement will try to tell you that God has removed his spirit from you. The demon will try to tell you that God doesn't love you because of a past sin or a present dilemma. But the Word tells us in Romans 8:1 that there is no condemnation to those who are in the Lord.

Since your motive and heart is after God, God's love covers a multitude of sin. His grace covers a multitude of our setbacks. Does that give us a license to sin? Certainly not. But it will bring us out of the depression of beating ourselves up for something God already knew would happen.

Lastly, God shows Elijah that he is not alone. There are thousands of prophets like him who have no bowed. There is Elisha, whom God makes provision for Elijah to meet. God does this because he knows that we are not meant to be alone. God may call us away for a wilderness experience, but for the most part, we are built to be be in relationship with one another. You need to free yourself today. Be free from the guilt of your setback. You are not alone. Thousands of us have been where you are right now. Thousands of soldiers are rooting for you, praying with you, and believing God with you. Don't give up! Don't throw in the towel! If you do, the demon will have the last word, and that was never the will of God concerning you.

Why Do SETBACKS happen in the first place?

True deliverance happens when you investigate why something happened in the first place. That way, we can prevent it from happening again. Oftentimes, God gives us a word before we go through anything. If we pay attention, we will already know that what He is taking us through won't take us out. We will already be prepared if He has to strip us of everything in order to attain something greater. If we listen to Him, He will get our attention the first time. He will point to the exit door when we need it.

So why do we have setbacks?

For the most part, we have them because we leave God out of our plans. We have goals and we have vision, but our goals will disappoint us if God is not included in them. There is no point in making a plan that you want to see happen, as if God does not exist. The future of our lives is in His hands. Why do we have setbacks? Because, sometimes, we try to be God. We try to act as if we are in control over our own lives and we are not. It's good to have plans. But the Lord orders our steps. What we will become ten years from now, one year from now, or 24 hours from now is all up to God's sovereign knowledge. He knows all. He leads us into all truth. So why not trust him with our plans? Why not put him in the center of your goals? If you want to avoid another setback, seek him first. That way, all these other things will be added unto you.

Why do we have setbacks? Because, sometimes, we try to be God.

And Jesus saith unto them, All ye shall be offended because of me this night: for it is written, I will smite the shepherd, and the sheep shall be scattered. But after that I am risen, I will go before you into Galilee
Mark 14:27-28

The second reason setbacks happen is because we don't truly know how to trust God yet. If God allows everything to be scattered and lost, we must learn to focus on the promise. He promises to make us better than before. He promises that we are more than conquerors. He promises that weeping may endure for a night. He promises to be our rock and fortress. He promises to be the way out of no way, but, oftentimes, we let our offenses cloud our promise. If God promises that He will make you better than you were before, nothing you experience today will cause you to lose your mind tomorrow. God has anointed you to survive every attack you have gone through. God prophesies the ending before the beginning. Consider these verses in Mark 14:29-31:

But Peter said unto him, Although all shall be offended, yet will not I. And Jesus saith unto him, Verily I say unto thee, That this day, even in this night, before the cock crow twice, thou shalt deny me thrice. But he spake the more vehemently, If I should die with thee, I will not deny thee in any wise. Likewise also said they all.

Peter was offended because Jesus accused him of denying Him. God knew from the very beginning that Peter would have a setback. Peter was busy trying to tell God how faithful he was. He reminded Jesus that He was with him in the storm. He reminded Jesus of his accolades and resume. Jesus didn't need Peter to remind him of anything. Just like with us. He doesn't need us to lay out our degrees on the table. He doesn't need our tithing record. God knows afar off, and just because we serve him, doesn't mean we won't have a setback. What Peter didn't know was that God knew beyond his today. He knew Peter would deny him today, but deliver others tomorrow. God knew that Peter would be a key part of the early church years later. The point is this: God sees beyond our setback moments. We can't get stuck on what we think we can control. We can't control the Creator. We are only the creation. The Creator has control over us. The day you will be free is the day you will take the limits off of God, and let God be God over your life.

Even Christ had a SETBACK moment

And they came to a place which was named Gethsemane: and he saith to his disciples, Sit ye here, while I shall pray. And he taketh with him Peter and James and John, and began to be sore amazed, and to be very heavy; And saith unto them, My soul is exceeding sorrowful unto death: tarry ye here, and watch. And he went forward a little, and fell on the ground, and prayed that, if it were possible, the hour might pass from him. And he said, Abba, Father, all things are possible unto thee; take away this cup from me: nevertheless not what I will, but what thou wilt.
Mark 14:32-36

At this point in the Scripture, Jesus is going through agony and depression. He is lonely. He is about to undergo events that will save the whole world. He is caring for people that don't care about Him. He is the only one doing good and He knows that people are taking him for granted. This is the lowest in spirit that the scriptures reveal about Jesus. He wants to abort the whole mission. He wants to backslide on the Father's mission.

These verses free me from trying to be perfect all of the time. Why? Because Even Christ had a SETBACK moment. Notice: it is possible to have a setback moment and not sin. It is possible to have a moment, but don't let your moment build a monument. Don't let your moment have a permanent marker in the timeline of your life. We all have doubts. We all have questions. God will take us through seasons that we don't necessarily understand. But if we respond "nevertheless, not what I will, but what thou wilt," we will quickly transition from a setback to a comeback.

It's like the wrestling matches or the boxing matches we watch on television. Usually, the fighter who is weakest in the beginning will turn out to be the strongest in the end. It's all about a mentality change. When you realize that this fight is connected to your family's financial sustenance, you find the power to get up and keep fighting. When you realize the lives attached to your spiritual boxing match, you will receive the strength to stand to your feet and keep fighting. You are not fighting alone, Elijah. You are not fighting alone, preacher. You are not fighting alone, nurse or doctor or lawyer. Jesus is in the courtroom with you. He is on the surgery table with you. There is no reason to fear, because your comeback has been orchestrated by God. Your comeback is a promise that God has made you. And that's reason enough to praise him!

> ***God will take us through seasons that we don't necessarily understand.***

Praise the Lord in the midst of your setback. Praise the Lord in the midst of your turmoil. Every setback was a setup to bring you to the forefront. Every moment of discouragement was designed to help you minister to those who are on the verge of suicide. If you hadn't gone through your Gethsemane experience, you wouldn't have an encouraging Word in your mouth for the broken branches in the garden. Change your perception and praise God through it all! When you look up and see where God has brought you from, you will learn to thank God for every moment you experienced in ministry. All of it has been orchestrated by God to strengthen you, not to destroy you!

Come back... and stay back!

Chapter Nine

From Once Upon A Time to Happily Ever After

Then cometh he to a city of Samaria, which is called Sychar, near to the parcel of ground that Jacob gave to his son Joseph. Now Jacob's well was there. Jesus therefore, being wearied with his journey, sat thus on the well: and it was about the sixth hour.

There cometh a woman of Samaria to draw water: Jesus saith unto her, Give me to drink. (For his disciples were gone away unto the city to buy meat.) Then saith the woman of Samaria unto him, How is it that thou, being a Jew, askest drink of me, which am a woman of Samaria? for the Jews have no dealings with the Samaritans.

Jesus answered and said unto her, If thou knewest the gift of God, and who it is that saith to thee, Give me to drink; thou wouldest have asked of him, and he would have given thee living water. The woman saith unto him, Sir, thou hast nothing to draw with, and the well is deep: from whence then hast thou that living water? Art thou greater than our father Jacob, which gave us the well, and drank thereof himself, and his children, and his cattle?

Jesus answered and said unto her, Whosoever drinketh of this water shall thirst again: But whosoever drinketh of the water that I shall give him shall never thirst; but the water that I shall give him shall be in him a well of water springing up into everlasting life. The woman saith unto him, Sir, give me this water, that I thirst not, neither come hither to draw.

Jesus saith unto her, Go, call thy husband, and come hither. The woman answered and said, I have no husband. Jesus said unto her, Thou hast well said, I have no husband: For thou hast had five husbands; and he whom thou now hast is not thy husband: in that saidst

thou truly. The woman saith unto him, Sir, I perceive that thou art a prophet. Our fathers worshipped in this mountain; and ye say, that in Jerusalem is the place where men ought to worship.
John 4:5-20 (KJV)

I know you have probably never been arrested before. You're too holy for that. And I know you don't know ANYONE who has been arrested before. All of your friends speak in tongues and never sin.

You have the right to remain silent.

And if, per chance, you have been arrested, I know why you got arrested. I know some devilish cop caught you out in the middle of the day giving out tracts for Jesus Christ. They persecuted you for the name of Jesus! He locked you up for spreading the gospel, certainly not for any other heinous crime. All of you reading haven't been through real incarceration. I know you are too saved for that.

But let's just *pretend* you know someone who has been arrested before. Let's just imagine that we are watching an episode of "Law and Order" together. You know there is one thing that cops must do before they handcuff you. They are required by law to tell you what your rights are. As they are putting handcuffs on you, you hear them say:

You have the right to remain silent.

Anything you say can and will be used against you in a court of law.

You have the right to speak to an attorney, and to have an at-

torney present during any questioning.

If you cannot afford a lawyer, one will be provided for you at government expense.

With these four sentences, they let you know everything that you need to know. They tell you from the door, you have the right to say nothing at all or you have the right to seek help from a professional. They try to help us out but most times we don't listen. Most times we yell at the top of our lungs, or we scream and holler; and every word we say—including the profanity we spew out of our mouths—will be held in the court of law against us. They tell us our rights so that we don't ruin our lives.

The Righteous must know His/Her Rights

Knowing your rights is crucial. Many times, you will talk yourself into disaster if you don't know your rights. Many times, people will get over on you if you don't know your rights. Insurance companies make a lot of money because their customers don't know their rights. Doctors make exorbitant amounts of extra cash all because you don't read your prescription. You've got to know who you are and know what you are entitled to as a citizen of this country. If not, you'll try to pretend to be something that you're not...all because, you don't know your rights.

Many Christians are suffering worse than our American Citizens. Why? Because we don't know that we have the right to be happy. We don't think that we have a right to enjoy life and live in abundance. But I want to assure you as we complete this book: you do have a right to be happy. You do have a right to be free. Just because you're suffering today, doesn't mean you will suffer forever. Just because you've experienced pain in the past, doesn't mean you will be imprisoned by pain forever. You must know your rights. If you don't, you'll always settle for whatever your EX- feels like giving you.

Why be Holy and not Happy?

I want to talk about the state of being happy. It's a state of being. It's not a state of "becoming." You must be happy because true happiness is not motivated by a temporary event. True happiness flows from the river of joy that God has deposited inside of you. Why be holy and unhappy at the same time?

Many people look happy on the outside but they are very unhappy internally. They are miserable and moping. They are sad and unapproachable. They say they love God, but their faces tell a different story. They walk around with the "I don't want to be bothered face." Everything around them is a nuisance. If it's too much noise, they are complaining. If the baby is crying, they are yelling and screaming. They don't smile at anybody, and yet, they wonder why people don't engage them in conversation.

Usually the face tells the world what's going on with you internally. In most cases, people who are unhappy are hurting on the inside. People are going through so much that they become frustrated with themselves. They cannot perceive being happy anymore. They have memorized the drama of dysfunction, and they are used to the pain. To them, pain has become a good feeling. It is a familiar place. All of their lives, they've had to fight. So they think that the way to receive love is through fighting and arguing. They have a very twisted understanding of true joy in Jesus Christ—and the people who are suffering with this complex the most, are sitting on the pew next to you every Sunday!

WHAT DOES YOUR SOUL LOOK LIKE?

The Bible says in 3 John 1:2, "Beloved, I wish above all things that you may prosper and be in health, even as thy soul prospereth." The soul is a beautiful piece of our human make up, but I wonder... if I were to take a picture of your soul, what would it look like?

Who might we see you choking?

Who might we see you cussing out?

Who might we see you crying over?

Who might we see you worrying about?

What unresolved issues would we see in your soul?

Where your heart is, your mind and your emotions live. Your soul is the centerpiece of your feelings. It is the place where we see the tenderness of your inner being. Every decision derives from a broken soul or a whole soul; a healthy soul or an unhealthy soul. What good would it be to have all the stuff in the world and your soul is dying a slow and invisible death? You have a right to be happy.

True happiness is when you look into the mirror and you like what you see.

You may be married with children, a beautiful home and a Mercedes Benz to match. But I've got news for you: stuff does not equal happiness. Once you get what you thought you wanted materially, you still may find yourself unhappy. And now, the only thing left to do is spread your doom and gloom to those around you. Misery loves company. Unhappy people will try to make happy people unhappy.

Listen to the news.

There are more rich people committing suicide now than ever before. They aren't happy. They have obtained wealth in the eyes of man, but their soul is broken, wounded, and empty. Why would you chase after things that don't want to chase after you? Your soul is longing for the richness of God's mercy. Your soul is longing for a place that only God can fill.

Some people measure happiness by what other people say. But true happiness comes from within you. True happiness is when you look in the mirror and you like what you see. Scars and all. Wrinkles and all. Weight and all. You don't need the validation of others. You appreciate it, but you don't need it to live. You can live off of your own compliments. You can take yourself out to a movie if there is no one to go with you. You can treat yourself to a spa if nobody else wants to go. Happiness is found in the completion of self-assurance. When God loves you and you love yourself, that is all you need to be happy.

DON'T BASE YOUR LIFE ON TV

We buy into a false idea of happiness when we compare our lives to the reality shows on television. Don't you realize that people are hired to entertain you? Any form of entertainment is an embellished version of the truth. Don't base your life and self-worth on the delusion of a TV screen. You are bigger than that. You are more beautiful than you realize. You are more important than that. Actors are paid high salaries to pretend. They are not the people they portray. They are only performing a role for service. It's work-for-hire.

If you compare yourself to the actors on television, you ruin your value. You don't see who God made you to be. You let the fantasy become your non-fiction and you will always find yourself "less than" something that has been made up, cleaned up, airbrushed, or graphically manipulated.

That's the one issue I have with people who would rather

watch The Word Network, TBN, or any other Christian Television Broadcast station instead of going to church. When we watch others worship on television, we get a false sense of community. We need to experience God for ourselves. The church has a very bad habit of presenting something way "up here" and yet living way "down here." We preach from high pulpits, but we live in the pits. We talk about security in God but we are the most insecure people in the world. We are imbalanced. We have bought into the TV delusion. Being happy is a product of feeling good about yourself. Don't let people control you like a thermostat. The only influence that matters is God. After Him, everyone else will have to adjust to you.

CONQUERING YOUR FAILURES!

Happiness is achieved when you feel good about the things in your life. Happiness is not popularity. Happiness is not a salary. Your kids can tell when you are really happy or when you are just acting. They can tell when we are going through the motions. You slam things around the house, you curse your loved ones out, you kick the cat and slam the door on the dog. Chances are, you are unhappy.

A large part of that happiness is rooted in failure. You feel like you haven't accomplished enough. You have a fear of failure or your life may have taken a few unexpected turns. But in the end, you win! In the end, God has ordered your steps. In the end, there must be one reason to be grateful for the bigger picture.

This goes back to the very beginning of the book. Don't get upset if you don't get what you want. Make sure that what you desire from God is in the will of God in the first place. He says "no" to us when He recognizes that this thing will pull us further away from him. Meanwhile, the devil puts a numbing and fearful attitude on you. He makes you afraid of stepping outside your boundaries. He's working against you so that you cannot accomplish what you want to accomplish. I know you have tried it before and it did not work, but if God has willed for you to succeed, you will succeed. I can't tell you the countless stories I've heard of singers who got rejected dozens of time before they made it big; or authors who were denied publishing rights until the 25th publisher gave them a chance. If you know your rights, you will chase your dreams. Don't let your history stop your destiny. Chase after your dreams, even if you are rejected time and time again.

...wherever you see fear, know that the devil is somewhere lurking around.

God has not given you the spirit of fear. So wherever you see fear, know that the devil is somewhere lurking around. He tries to put fear in our lives so that fear can birth unhappiness. And happiness will birth stagnation. And all of this will birth doubt and delay. Figure out the cycle so that you can avoid the snares of the enemy. God has not given you fear. So don't accept it. Instead, say to yourself, "I know my rights. Fear does not belong to me. It is not a part of me. I will come out of this." Tell yourself that you are going to be happy. No matter what mistakes you've made, declare that you will come out of this rut. I don't care what it looks like. You may have tripped and fallen. You may have had people scoff in your face to make a mockery of what you did. But declare to yourself "I will be happy. I am determined to have peace." Today is going to be your launching day toward destiny after you finally free yourself from the opinions of others.

I AM MY WORST CRITIC!

The true test of a real praiser is when you become your own worst critic. When you go home and say, "What was wrong with me? What was I thinking? How stupid am I! I should have known better." These are good self-evaluators. You aren't waiting for someone else to tell you what you already know. You aren't in denial. You can't blame anyone else but yourself. And when you finally come to yourself, you can get up quicker and move forward! You must learn to be your own critic. Don't let people spew negativity in your face. Examine yourself. Do the hard work of self-inventory. Clean up the areas that need cleaning and make a declaration to move on and make better decisions.

The unhappiest people in the world are unhappy because they look for others to make them happy. They search outside of themselves for the source of their happiness. They need for me to speak a Word over them in order for them to smile. They need an external object to make them internally secure. But this is the wrong road to go down. People cannot produce happiness within you. They have no right creating the terms and conditions of your happiness. True happiness does not begin around you. Happiness begins inside of you.

It is not flowers being brought to you. It is allowing the seed of the flower to grow inside you until you blossom and those around you say, "Look how beautiful you are!" You've got to criticize yourself. Grow yourself. Love on yourself. Low self-esteem will rob you of happiness. Feeling unworthy will steal the joy you deserve to experience in life. You must decide that you are the gift, you are a present, you are a flower, you are a lovely fragrance. You smell good. You look good and you are good. Not because of anybody else. But simply because of the relationship you and God have together.

Joy is Available. How Bad do YOU want it?

The joy of the lord becomes your strength. This is a familiar scripture, but the revelation of this verse is important if you want to be happy. God is not handing out joy. He is not auctioning joy out to the highest bidder. God says, "if you give me joy, I will give you strength." If you give God praise, He will give you power. If you exchange your will for His, He will give you direction. Joy is available. Happiness is attainable. But you've got to know your rights. We give our joy to Him and he replenishes us with strength. It works like a vending machine. The items are available for purchase, but you've got to put something in to get something out. When we praise him, we exchange our sorrow for joy. When we praise him, He turns our mourning into dancing. When we magnify Him, we show God how valuable He is to us. We are not meant to be sad and somber. We are designed to praise him and give all glory back to Him.

Even when others forsake you, He gives you the staying power and strength not to lose your sanity.

But the question is: how bad do you want it? How bad do you want the joy you've been asking God for? The level of praise we give him will reveal the desire we have to receive joy from the Lord. Understand that every time you give God praise, it will activate the joy. Praise gives us the joy that never expires; the joy that outlasts the sadness of today's bad news. You can go through dreadful situations, you can have a loved one leave you, you can have your husband or wife walk out on you, and still they have not taken your joy. You may have been their joy, but Jesus is your joy! Jesus is your rock. Even when others forsake you, He gives you the staying power and strength not to lose your sanity. If God hasn't left you, the joy of the Lord is still with you!

A Remedy for Pain

The next most popular reason people remain unhappy is because they refuse to let go of their past pain. Each chapter in this book has helped us to see our pain differently. It's hard to say goodbye, but once you do it, you've got to let go of the pain and turn it into a gain. Dismiss and replace. Your future is giving your past an eviction notice. You are stretching out now more than you ever have before. You tripped up—yes. You messed up—yes. But don't let the devil steal your victory.

I have a remedy for getting rid of the pain of the past. It's three simple things that you need to do.

Acknowledge your pain

Release it into the atmosphere

Thank god for your rain.

I know without a doubt in my mind that God is about to rain on you. Anytime the rain is about to come, the clouds get full. The earth gets dark. The day looks like night. And the sound of thunder will scare you into thinking God is mad at you. But know your rights! God promised to open up the window of heaven and pour out a blessing that you won't have room to receive. Acknowledge the pain. That way, your pain can't tell you what to do with your purpose. Release it into the atmosphere. Whether it is unforgiveness, anger, strife, envy—whatever it is, release it. When you let it go, God can take care of it and handle it all! Third, thank God for the rain. Even though you can't see it, thank God for what God is going to do in faith. Praise him for what you can't see but you know is there. Thank God for the graduation ceremony before you finish your first semester. Thank God for the promotion before you start your first day of work. Thank God for the case being dismissed even before you go to court. Thank God for the rain. The rain is a sign that God is with you. The rain is a symbol that God wants you to rejoice. Dance in the rain! Praise in the rain. God is about to rain out his blessings upon you. Just make sure you hands are empty of the EX so that you will have room to receive his abundance.

Jesus was the BLESSING, and the Woman didn't see it!

If the woman in the highlighted verse in John 4 had read this book, she would've recognized Jesus from the moment he sat down at the well. But she couldn't see the rain because she was stuck in religion. The bible says that Jesus was making a special trip to Galilee. In order to get there, he had to go through Samaria. This is a different place. It isn't where Jesus' folks usually hang out. So of course, Jesus looks suspect. He appears to be flirting with this woman. It looks like, from the outside looking in, that Jesus is trying to court this lady. He is single. So, many people see Jacob's well as the "flirting well."

In history, the well was a meeting place. It was a landmark for people to get to know one another. You know, like some of you who come to church for a meeting place and not a time to worship.

You think you can hook up with certain people, or exchange business cards with potential clients. Why? Because you have turned the church into the well. You have made God's house of worship into your match.com. At the well is where Jacob met his wife Rachel. So this is why they call it Jacob's well. This woman has a history. She knows what people usually do at the well, so when she sees Jesus, she thinks he is just any other guy. Jesus sits there and asked the woman for a drink of water. To her, this is a pick up line. To Jesus, this in an introduction to her license of eternal happiness.

Jesus is crossing the boundaries. He is doing this with you.

Jesus says, "Give me some water girl."

She responds, "Well you don't have anything to draw with."

He speaks to her but the woman is confused. She knows that Jesus shouldn't even be talking to a Samaritan woman. He is a Jew and she is not. Normally, Jews have no dealings with Samaritans. All this time, Jesus is using his conversation to preach a new message of worship. But she's so stuck in religion that she misses the rain.

Jesus is crossing the boundaries. He is doing this with you. He was supposed to pass her over. He was supposed to pass you over. But grace and mercy allowed him to stop by your neighborhood and deliver you from the hand of the enemy. Jesus is all about sitting with sinners and eating with them. His goal for coming to earth was not for the saved but for the lost.

The Bible says that he looks at her, and he asks for water. She continues to insist that she is not supposed to give him water, so Jesus decides to change the subject. He tells her to go get her husband. She claims not to have anybody. He looks at her and tells her that she's lying. He knows she is lying. Just like some of the people I pastor every week. I know you have a sugar daddy on the side. Stop lying. I know you're pimping on the side. Stop lying. I know you have a part time personality on the side. Stop lying.

Jesus knows you! Jesus knows me! We ain't fooling nobody but ourselves. That's why he shows up at the well. He shows up where we once met our EX, so that he can change our lives. He's come to get our lives in order once and for all.

Jesus exposes her with this truth, "You don't only have one husband. You have had five husbands." This means that she has been around the block. She must've been related to Elizabeth Taylor because she's had quite a few husbands, and the man she is living with now is a "husband" with benefits but no commitment.

Let me pause right there and tell my young ladies: stop giving these men your benefits without commitment. You are beautiful and you are worth the wait. If he wants your benefits, tell him to put a ring on it. Tell him to marry you at the well, don't just take your number and drink your water without working for it.

Jesus catches her in a bind. He wants her to know about the seventh man. The seventh man will give her peace. The other six have given her trouble. The seventh man will give her joy, even though the other six have polluted her mind with junk. The seventh man will give her eternal happiness. The six men have given her nothing but horrible memories of a wish-dream that wasn't there when she woke up. Jesus basically says to this woman, "I know what you need. These men have been giving you trouble. These men have not been able to satisfy the needs you have in your life. They may have paid your light bill, but they could not pay your emotional bill. They may have been able to help you get through some hard times, but where were they when you were about to lose your mind?" The water Jesus offers her is a lifetime package, full of free refills and overflow. It is the true and living water; the kind that will allow her never to thirst again. This water will never give out.

She still thinks he is flirting. But Jesus is not flirting. The water he speaks about is the water of life. She asks for him to give her this water. And Jesus reads her past, exposes her present, and frees her from making future mistakes. He tells her, in no uncertain terms, "Whatever you're holding onto. Let it go. It's too much. You can't handle it."

I leave you with these same words that Jesus told the woman at the well. Whatever husbands you are holding on to, let them go. Whatever Ex's have kept you locked in a state of non-productivity, release it and let it go. Make room for the rain. You deserve to be happy. You deserve to have your blessings and enjoy them, too. God is faithful to provide what we need when we need it. He can turn your "Once upon a time" into a "happily ever after." Now that you've matured; now that you've released your EX-factor, you are ready to experience the abundance of God's rain. Let the rain of His presence fall on you. Let the glory of His assurance minister to you. Even in times of weakness, God will be your strength. You deserve to be happy. There is so much greater for you later. You are walking toward your destiny, and God is with you! The greatest news you need to hear and know is that GOD IS WITH YOU! Never let your EX have a future again.

Contact the Author

Conferences, Motivational Speaking, Workshops

DeMarcus Pierson Ministries

Mailing Address:

202 N. Parkdale

Tyler, TX 75702

Website: www.demarcuspierson.com

Church Website: www.omegaMI.org

Email: omegaministries@peoplepc.com